Untamed Gospel

Untamed Gospel

*Protests, Poems and Prose
for the Christian Year*

Martyn Percy
with
Nigel Biggar
Jamie Coats
Jim Cotter
Sarah Foot
Carol Harrison
Sylvia Sands
Graham Ward

© The Contributors 2017

First published in 2017 by the Canterbury Press Norwich
Editorial office
3rd Floor, Invicta House
108–114 Golden Lane
London EC1Y 0TG, UK

Canterbury Press is an imprint of Hymns Ancient & Modern Ltd
(a registered charity)

Hymns Ancient & Modern® is a registered trademark of
Hymns Ancient & Modern Ltd
13A Hellesdon Park Road, Norwich,
Norfolk NR6 5DR, UK

www.canterburypress.co.uk

British Library Cataloguing in Publication data

A catalogue record for this book is available
from the British Library

978 1 84825 990 4

Typeset by Regent Typesetting
Printed and bound in Great Britain by
CPI Group (UK) Ltd

Contents

Part 2 Sermons and Homilies for the Christian Year

Story: In the Beginning, the Word *Martyn Percy*

Part 3 Sermons and Homilies for Other Occasions

For Dan and Nicola –
Two Faithful and Untamed Ministers of the Gospel

Introduction

This new text complements *The Bright Field* and *Darkness Yielding*,[1] and offers meditations, short reflections, stories and poems covering the Christian year. These relate to our time – an age of anger, austerity, assertion and anxiety. The poems and reflections carry an intentional edge, mindful of the political dimensions preached and proclaimed in the ministry of Jesus, and his inauguration of the reign of the kingdom of God.

As with *The Bright Field*, the content of the book is structured around *meze* – a traditional range of Middle Eastern foods and appetizers that can be shared among friends dining together. The *meze* motif is deliberate. Some of the meditations and reflections are designed to be studied and discussed and, as such, are more substantial. Others are shorter and pithier, and can be grazed upon for more individual study. The variety offered is key to how the book can be used and read.

There are over 40 sections to dwell on, as well as stories, poems and prose. Like *Darkness Yielding* and *The Bright Field*, the authors have given a rather free range to their imaginations in writing these aids to reflection. They cover the life of Jesus, with homilies for the ascension, transfiguration and other feasts – as well as tackling more contemporary issues in the life of the Church.

I am sincerely grateful to my Canon Professor colleagues from Christ Church Oxford – Nigel Biggar, Sarah Foot, Carol Harrison and Graham Ward – for allowing me to use their material in this volume. Their stimulating preaching inspires thousands of visitors and worshippers every year. The Canon Professors of Christ Church hold almost unique roles in the academy and the Church.

They hold senior professorships in one of the world's leading faculties of Theology and Religious Studies, combining this with normal liturgical and pastoral duties in the Cathedral of Christ Church Oxford, as well as being full members of the Cathedral Chapter, and full members of the College Governing Body. I am hugely appreciative of their willingness – and the giving of their time – both to commit to this book, and for their collegiality and friendship.

It is good to be able to welcome and introduce the poetry of Jamie Coats in this anthology. Jamie is a layperson working for the Society of St John the Evangelist (SSJE) in the United States – an Anglican religious order of brothers. Jamie writes on contemporary monastic wisdom, and his work draws on Buddhist, Hindu and Christian traditions of meditation and silence. We reproduce his 'Candle Trilogy' towards the close of this volume.

It is a pleasure, once again, to be able to draw on material from Sylvia Sands and Jim Cotter. Sylvia's work has reached thousands of readers, and her poems have a poignant and prophetic tone that is rarely matched by other contemporary poets. It is a privilege to be able to feature her work again (she contributed to *Darkness Yielding* originally, first published some 20 years ago, and now in its third edition).

Jim Cotter died in the midst of the busyness of Holy Week in 2014. His liturgies and prayers have been among the most influential aids to reflection produced by anyone in his generation. Jim was a poet-priest – someone for whom words were as important as the air we breathe. He wrote prayers, as one obituary put it, 'in which unicorns danced'.

Jim was instrumental in the bringing together of *Darkness Yielding*, many years ago. Jim was a gay priest, and he often talked openly about the importance of gay clergy being out, and living in the open as normal. He was a natural radical and disturber, as well as a caring consoler. Moreover, his prayers and reflections underline how much of a visionary and a prophet he was. Many readers still have copies of his night prayers sitting beside their beds. A typical prayer of Jim's was:

God be in my gut and in my feeling
God be in my bowels and in my forgiving
God be in my loins and in my swiving
God be in my lungs and in my breathing
God be in my heart and in my loving
God be in my skin and in my touching
God be in my flesh and in my yearning
God be in my blood and in my living
God be in my bones and in my dying
God be at my end and at my reviving

Our hope, as authors, is that the reflections, homilies and poems in this volume will enrich the spiritual lives of readers, accompanying them in their daily discipleship. Moreover, that the meditations and musings that follow will help us all awaken to the challenges of being a Christian in this age, renewing our vocation to enable the coming of the kingdom of God in our time.

THE VERY REVD PROFESSOR MARTYN PERCY

Dean, Christ Church Oxford,
Passiontide 2017

Part 1

Untamed Gospel: Protests and Promptings

Wisdom and counter-intuition

Martyn Percy

For those of you who are unfamiliar with Radio 4's enduring and established programme *I'm Sorry I Haven't a Clue*, it bills itself as '*The* antidote to panel games', and sets two teams 'some silly things to do', which somehow manages to fill half an hour with wit and humour. I have been hooked on the programme since I first heard it. Games such as 'Mornington Crescent' and 'One Song to the Tune of Another' never fail to inspire, and I have often thought that churches could do their own version: one hymn to the tune of another, for instance.

But for me it is the final round that is often the best: can the teams suggest novels suitable for plumbers? Or films likely to appeal to undertakers? And so forth. *I'm Sorry I Haven't a Clue* works because it blends irony with the peculiarly English fondness for what we might term 'high nonsense', and the result is half an hour of intelligent jokes.

In a similar vein, I invite you to contemplate the joys of *Movie Antonyms*. The object of the game is to invent film titles that don't quite cut the mustard: *The Under-performing Seven*; *Lassie, Get Lost*; *Lawrence of Suburbia*; *Decent Offer*; *Dinner at Ratners*; and so forth. Such a game works because it plays with, and characterizes, opposites; it offers us incongruous contrasts. We can see a similar pattern in the Bible. Jesus is supposed to be wise. But he creates mayhem in the temple, and upsets everyone going about their lawful trading in dubious religious tat. And he goes the whole hog too, driving them out with a whip that he made himself. Jesus doesn't do things by halves.

It seems to me to be quite important to try and comprehend what the lectionary might be trying to get across to us, by linking the account of the vision for the new heaven and earth from Revelation, the writer of Hebrews writing about sacrifice, and then Jesus' apparent rush of blood to the head in this temple story – where he not only behaves like a teenager in line for an anti-social behaviour order, but also goes on to claim the temple for his own ends.

But before I get to the link between these events, here's another and different kind of interesting riddle. Which is more important: that the right people do the wrong things, or the wrong people do the right things? The answer depends, I suspect, on where you are standing. From the point of view of the Church, the right people doing the wrong things is 'where it's at'. The efficacy of the sacraments does not depend on the effectiveness or competency of the celebrant. The vicar can, in other words, make a dog's breakfast of the baptism or the Eucharist – but he or she is the right person to do it, even if that person gets it wrong. A layperson doing it and getting it right won't do – that's wrong.

But as at least one theologian has reminded us, in the battles between Jesus and the Church, the latter might be ahead on points, but it is still fighting a war it cannot ultimately win. The right people do the wrong things; the wrong people do the right stuff. And it is clear what Jesus thinks: the tax-collectors and the prostitutes will get to heaven before the apparently righteous. The wrong kind of people doing the right kind of stuff is where Scripture seems to cast its vote.

In Matthew's Gospel there is a playful mull on Jesus' apparent wisdom and foolishness. Jesus spends much of his ministry being cast not as a hero, but as a bit of a nutcase. His words and works are prejudged, because even in first-century Palestine the social and theological construction of reality seems to prejudice many people's perceptions.

To casual onlookers, turning out the traders from the temple is a silly thing to do: they don't mean any harm, do they? And of course we all know that the price of pigeons is double what you pay outside the temple. We accept this. Jesus, in contrast, does not and, as in so many cases, behaves rather badly. Behold! He eats and drinks with a bad crowd; finds himself portrayed as a glutton and a drunkard. It is a no-win situation. But Jesus says, somewhat cryptically: 'wisdom is vindicated by her deeds' (Matthew 11.19).

Wisdom, then, is the link – because the second part of Matthew's Gospel outlines how the seemingly wise and righteous appear unable to see what is in front of their noses, while the apparently foolish and unrighteous seem to have perceived it. In John Hull's profound book *In the Beginning There Was Darkness: A Blind Person's Conversations with the Bible*,[2] he meditates upon the themes of sight and blindness and light and darkness that abound in Scripture. The theme of the book is to challenge what he calls 'the sighted monopoly of interpretation' that so often governs our readings of the Scriptures.

John Hull's meditations as a blind person, *feeling*, imagining and thinking his way through Scripture, as it were, start to make readers think that they may be missing something because they actually 'see' too much. Our eyes can play tricks on us. But the person who knows that God is both beyond the darkness and the light has already begun to perceive something deeper and richer than most sighted persons can ever begin to understand. In the presence of God we are actually all blind, for his light is too dazzling; and his darkness is too deep. To not 'see', therefore, is not necessarily to be handicapped, for there can be substantial gains in such perception.

John, who begins his Gospel in darkness, with the light of the world to come, would doubtless concur with this kind of thinking because his 'life' of Jesus is full of such subtle interplay. Jesus exhorts his followers to be fools for his sake: to not accept what the world sees as rational, but rather peer deeper into reality; to see that God's foolishness is brighter than the wisdom of the world. How else, after all, can we explain Jesus' invitation to 'all who are burdened and heavy-laden' to 'come' to him; to move at a point when we are arguably already exhausted? His claim at this juncture is that he will give us rest.

How will this be done? Oddly, by taking on another weight – namely, a yoke. Yet Jesus is careful to add that we will find this yoke easy and light, so on the surface the invitation seems foolish. That is, of course, until we step into the kinds of weights and harness that are offered. It is only at this point that wisdom is found in apparent foolishness. The extra weight actually lightens the load. This is, as Paul might say, 'God's foolishness that is wider than human wisdom'. It doesn't make sense – but God's weakness is stronger than human strength.

So Jesus' action in the temple – reckless, violent and apparently intemperate – in actuality contains quite a strong message. It conveys wisdom: saying that sometimes breaking our frames of reference with such sharpness is the only way to get us to see how foolish we have been. This is the key to understanding the incident: this is about breaking paradigms. So there was really no point at all in trading up from a pigeon to a dove. Neither sacrifice would bring people closer to God; they were wasting their money. There was no point in going for the 'three for two' offer on goats, or the 'buy one get one free' offer on lambs.

Much of the gospel is about being reconciled to what has been hidden, and looking deeper into what has been revealed, and to seeing beyond the apparently obvious: to find the wisdom in apparent folly. This is why Jesus' 'anger' in the gospel is so interesting, for it seems not to be a hot, quick, irrational 'snap'; but rather a cold and calculating anger.

There is a difference between hot anger and cold – perhaps righteous – anger. Jesus actually went away and *made* the whips of cords. This is a cold premeditated attack, not a rush of blood to the head. He has, as the Epistle to James puts it, 'been slow to anger'; but now he's got there, and he's meting out punishment.

As Harvey Cox noted in *On Not Leaving it to the Snake*,[3] the first and original sin is not disobedience. It is, rather, indifference. We can no longer ignore the pain and alienation that others in the Church experience – and especially when this is *because* of the Church. Indifference is pitiful, and it is the enemy of compassion.

So there are three things we can say in conclusion. First, what is Jesus so upset about in the temple? It seems to me that it lies in assumptions: about the 'natural order of things'; about status and privilege; about possessions; about prevailing wisdom. This is, in other words, un-examined lives and practices lived in unexamined contexts. Everyone is blind. Jesus' action forces us to confront the futile sight before us, his anger forces us to look again. I like Lytta Bassett's excellent book *Holy Anger: Jacob, Job, Jesus*,[4] which offers a profound theological excavation of these themes.

Second, the story chides us all for that most simple of venial sins: overlooking. The trading has been happening for donkey's years. It is simply part of the furniture; it barely merits a look, let alone comment. Jesus, of course, always looks deeper. But the lesson of the story is that, having looked within us with such penetration, his gaze then often shifts – to those who are 'below' us – in other words, those with less wealth, health, intelligence, conversation, social skills, life.

Third, the besetting sin is that the temple traders appear to accept the status quo, and the story has one thing to say about this: don't. Don't accept that a simple small gesture can't ripple out and begin to change things. Don't accept, wearily, that we can't make a difference – we can. Sometimes the change can be radical, but more often than not the change comes about through small steps – and we need to be ready for both.

Either way, *I'm Sorry I Haven't a Clue* won't do for disciples. Just as the great game show turns knowledge and logic on its head, and often seems to be nonsense, so we are, sometimes, asked to be fools for Christ. But our course is set by something deeper: wisdom. Foolishness to the world for sure, but in that foolishness is Christ, the power and wisdom of God.

Human evolution to 'higher things'

Nigel Biggar

In Advent we look forward to God's coming, and specifically to his coming among us and entering our condition – his incarnation in Jesus. We look forward to it because the divine incarnation is a dramatic sign that God identifies with us, that he is on our side, that he wants to rescue us. It is a sign of the lengths to which

God's love will go. The incarnation, then, is important for our salvation.

But it's also important for something else – namely, our nature – and it's this I want to focus on here. The incarnation implies that human nature is capable of divinity. To use the language of St Paul in the Epistle to the Colossians, human nature is capable of 'things above' (Colossians 3.1). In this respect, then, the incarnation is a confirmation and intensification of the famous notion in Genesis 1 – namely, that human beings are made 'in the image of God' (Genesis 1.27).

In the course of Jewish and Christian history this phrase has been interpreted to mean a variety of things. But it is clear from the text that it means, at the very least, that human beings are the climax of God's creating and that they stand at the very apex of the created world. More substantively, in the light of the story that follows in Genesis 2 and 3, being made in God's image involves being capable of entering into friendship with God and of finding fulfilment therein.

This idea of human beings made in God's image, confirmed and intensified by God's coming among us and taking on human flesh in the incarnation, is the basis of a Christian humanism – of a theologically grounded understanding of the special dignity and high calling of human beings.

However, this Christian humanism – and indeed, any other kind of humanism – is fundamentally challenged and undermined by the popular interpretation of Charles Darwin's theory of natural evolution – the kind of interpretation now regularly given voice in public discourse. As this view has it, human motivation is *reducible* to that of the primitive forms of life from which we have evolved. What drives us, basically, is the impulse or desire for self-preservation at some level. This argument states that since our genes are selfish, so, basically and naturally, are we. For sure, we sometimes appear to be altruistic, but that's all it is: appearance. Our acts of co-operation and generosity, according to this viewpoint, are only more shrewd expressions of self-interestedness. Our capability of higher things is an illusion.

Quite why such a view is so popular, especially among decent, liberal people, is perplexing, since its implications for human dignity become so grim and depressing – and I don't for a moment suppose that many of those who espouse it actually live by it.

So why do they espouse it at all? I suspect that the deepest reason lies in a determined, wilful rejection of spiritual realities, made on the sinful, typically adolescent, and false assumption that external claims suffocate human freedom and flourishing.

Darwinists would argue, I imagine, that their view of human beings is determined simply by scientific reasoning, but I doubt that on empirical grounds. I don't actually think that Darwinist anti-humanism *is* determined by science – that is, by logic applied to empirical data. Rather, I think it's generated by the *choice* to read evolutionary science in terms of materialist philosophy, most notably that of Thomas Hobbes.

Writing in the light of the political conflict and then terrible Civil War that afflicted England in the 1640s, Thomas Hobbes chose as his disillusioned starting point for thinking about social and political life a supposedly original 'state of nature'. Here human life, in Hobbes' phrase, is famously 'solitary, poor, nasty, brutish, and short', because social relations comprise a war of all against all, since human beings are individualistic atoms, driven first and last by the fear of pain and death.

But this cynical reading of human conduct and motivation is actually quite *un*realistic. Hobbes articulated his disillusionment from the academic distance and armchair safety of Paris. Meanwhile, his friend Lucius Carey, Viscount Falkland, Lord of the manor of Great Tew just north of Oxford, and amateur theologian, was demonstrating that not even England's internecine bloodbath bottled down to the mythical 'state of nature'. Towards the end of the battle of Edgehill, just north of Banbury, in 1642, Falkland interposed himself between his own victorious royalist comrades on the one hand, and a sorry group of surrendered parliamentarians on the other, in order to stop the former from slaughtering the latter. That is, he transcended his own drive for self-preservation and fear of death to save others. And these others were not his kin – they were not even members of his political group. More to the point, they weren't just strangers; they were the actual enemy.

That's one piece of empirical evidence that contradicts the

materialist reading of evolutionary science – an instance of a human being subordinating the desire for self-preservation to his love for others, even risking the former for the latter. And it's by no means unique. After all, think Jesus.

Darwinists, of course, try to explain this away by arguing that Falkland's conduct was driven at a deeper level by selfish motives. But in my view such explanations are invariably either laughably tortured or unprovable, or both. Sometimes it just makes more sense to trust the appearances of something.

My second piece of evidence takes us to the National Museum of Slovenia in Ljubljana. The Museum's prize exhibit is the four-and-a-half-inch section of bone that belonged to the femur of a cave-bear. On it are two almost identical holes. Experts have determined that these were not caused by the teeth of another animal; rather, they were deliberately carved by a human being. Or, to be more exact, they were created by a Neanderthal about 50,000 years ago.

Why? Well, it seems that in between a Neanderthal's stereo-typical hunting and copulating, he fancied carving himself a flute. That is to say, 50,000 years ago a very primitive human being found himself driven not just by the desire to preserve himself or to reproduce, but also by the desire to experience the beauty of music and the satisfaction of playing it. Even Neanderthal man, our now extinct cousin, was evidently capable of higher things.

The empirical evidence is, I think, that human beings have evolved morally to the point where they are capable of appreciat-ing and desiring a much wider range of valuable things – a much wider range of goods – than could the forms of life from which we originated. Not only the preservation and reproduction of phys-ical life, but also non-material, spiritual goods such as beauty, playfulness, justice and friendship with God. What is more, our appreciation of these spiritual goods is such that we sometimes prefer higher things to lower ones, and even risk or sacrifice the lower for the sake of the higher. As did Viscount Falkland; as did Jesus.

The remarkable irony that this view exposes is that a philo-sophically materialist reading of the scientific theory of natural evolution doesn't have us evolve morally at all: it holds that our values, interests and motives are basically the same as they always were. Morally, we remain stuck at our origins.

By contrast, a Christian humanist reading of natural evolution, which takes the anthropological and historical evidence seriously and isn't constrained by atheistic dogma to twist and distort it to fit materialist prejudice, is able to recognize that we humans really have evolved morally. We are not, morally speaking, reducible to our origins. We have become capable of higher things, capable of appreciating a wider range of goods, capable of investing ourselves in non-material, spiritual goods – capable, indeed, of desiring and receiving the Advent of divinity.

A gospel according to risk management, health and safety?

Martyn Percy

> But [Jesus] turned and said to Peter, 'Get behind me, Satan! You are a stumbling-block to me; for you are setting your mind not on divine things but on human things.' Then Jesus told his disciples, 'If any want to become my followers, let them deny themselves and take up their cross and follow me. For those who want to save their life will lose it, and those who lose their life for my sake will find it.' (Matthew 16.23–25)

The following is from an article in the *Church Times*:

> Two survivors of clerical abuse have praised the Dean and Chapter of Christ Church, Oxford, for facilitating their protest at the consecration of Dr Steven Croft as Bishop of Oxford last Friday. One of the protestors, 'Michael', has accused Dr Croft and others in the hierarchy of ignoring him when he told them that he was raped by a priest in the diocese of Bradford during the 1980s while a 16-year-old (News, 29 July). He was joined by 'Joe', who last year won an apology and damages for an assault by the former Chancellor of three dioceses, the Revd Garth Moore, and for the Church's subsequent response

(News, 4 December). On Friday, the two handed out leaflets to those attending the consecration [at Christ Church]. At one point, they were brought a plate of sandwiches ... The Dean, the Very Revd Professor Martyn Percy, had invited the pair back to Oxford to discuss issues surrounding safeguarding and the reporting of abuse, Joe said. He went on: 'So it was not only a very effective protest ... but was graciously received,' and managed to create potential for good dialogue.'[5]

There is a lot of talk today of 'safe spaces', 'no platforming' and 'risk aversion' in universities. Furthermore, quite recently there was an initiative driven by doubtless well-meaning managers and administrators that proposed to pre-vet all history lectures in case any of the events or ideologies studied caused undue distress to the students.

It is hard to imagine a history curriculum redacted of incidents and personalities that would result in zero-tolerance for the slightest pang of anguish. World War Two without the fighting, perhaps? Hiroshima without the bomb? Auschwitz, mentioning the efficient railways, but neglecting to mention the terminus of the death factories and camps? Marxism without brutality? Capitalism, but only the nice bits, without the 1930s Great Depression and the big spikes in suicide rates? History can be very upsetting, but history will only repeat itself if no one listened the first time around.

The incident described above in the extract from the *Church Times* really happened, and yet I do, in all seriousness, wonder why this is even reported in a newspaper. Why? Because the Church showed hospitality to strangers, which the gospel asks us to do. And we prayed for, and were kind to, those who might merely have disrupted a public act of worship, because the gospel expects much more of us.

It seemed obvious to me that, for protesters who had travelled many, many miles at their own expense, and would not have time to get lunch, or even know where to go for any food, that the obvious and right thing to do was to share our lunch with them – to break bread with them. To check on their dietary requirements, of course; and to ensure there was even a bowl of water for the dog they had brought with them. The little details matter. Cynics may of course say that this protest was killed with kindness; that our engagement was a PR-bluff.

But that is hardly the point here. It is the gospel that commands us to care for our sisters and brothers – all humanity – with hospitality and generosity, and without any motivation of personal or corporate gain. We are simply commanded to do it – because God loves humanity and also a cheerful giver.

Of course, I completely understand why it might be tempting to handle this incident with the protesters in a different way. Legal counsel might say it is unwise to meet with or engage with demonstrators, lest this open up a further opportunity for misunderstanding. Others may say it invalidates insurance policies; yet others may claim that this risks communications and public relations strategies. Suppose the encounter turns ugly, the argument goes, and the media capture it all? Some may go further, and suggest that by offering our food to strangers, there is a further health and safety risk with regard to diets and allergies. Yes, there are many good reasons to hold back hospitality.

But when we read the Parable of the Good Samaritan, we do not encounter the following. The Samaritan, for example, fretting about his own personal accident and travel insurance by voluntarily taking on the liability of a stranger in distress. Or of his bank intervening, to say that they will not underwrite the cost of the hostel expenses that the stranger might run up, as he has not been pre-vetted as a signatory on the Samaritan's account. Or the Samaritan, even for a second, wondering if the half-dead stranger he picks up at the roadside is part of an elaborate ruse or hoax designed to fleece the unwary of their possessions.

Nor do we read of my namesake – St Martin – pausing as he cuts his cloak in two to give half to a beggar who is cold and starving reflecting on how his personal possessions accidental damage waiver clause might now be invalid. He just cuts his cloak in two. Like the Samaritan, it is a pure and instinctual outpouring of compassion. It crosses boundaries. These gestures take deliberate risks. They are hardly reckless acts, but they do expose one human to another human's vulnerability and need. But that is the gospel, isn't it?

I do understand today why we might be risk aversive, and the value of diligence, prudent policies and collective responsibility, and the possibility of reputational damage and corporate jeopardy. I understand the need for managers to help us assess such risks, enabling us to have efficient systems that keep things contained and quarantined, and with good communications and public relations. I understand the need for child-protection policies.

But all such management – motivated out of concern for our health and safety – is surely there to serve us, not lead us? A health-and-safety-risk-aversive-safe-space-religion is not the gospel. Good management in such spheres can serve the Church, but it should never be allowed to lead it.

When Jesus teaches us about discipleship, he talks about risk; but he does not take the risk away. He warns us that we might die for this faith. He means this literally, not figuratively or metaphorically. We are to wash one another's feet too. No training is provided for this; we don't risk-assess the feet in advance before they come into our hands.

We are told to take up the cross, but the cross is heavy, and its daily carriage will cause repetitive strain and injury. But we can't be Christians without bearing this weight. We are here not to save and serve our own lives, but to lose them. So the gospel *is* risk, and to be a disciple and participate in the daily work of the kingdom of God is to be exposed to a world of risk.

That said, it is easy to understand why some senior clerics in the Church adopt risk-aversive stratagem: they are counselled to do so by their managers. But the gospel is not a risk-aversive, management-led enterprise. If that was what we thought we were doing when we signed up for Christianity, we didn't read the contract. In effect, the contract said we might lose our lives – and even if we don't, God would still like us to die to ourselves.

So let's stop colluding with the risk-aversive managers who think they are here to lead us. They're not. They are here to serve the Church, not lead it. We don't want the Church to be run by ecclesiocrats who keep setting us their numerical and financial targets in a gloomy climate of ecclesionomics. Nor is the kingdom of heaven to be a protectionist 'safe space' overseen by ecclesial managers. It is, rather, a project that needs courageous leadership:

a place of loving risk, openness and humanity, boundless generosity, encounter – and maybe even some danger. It is a place where we are to try and break bread with strangers, and even our enemies, if we are to see this kingdom come on earth – as it is in heaven.

Horror or glory: what's basic?

Nigel Biggar

The Thin Red Line[6] is a very unusual film. But the *most* unusual thing about it is that it is one of the most seriously religious films – perhaps even one of the most substantially Christian – ever made. It was released in 1999, shortly after *Saving Private Ryan*. Unlike *Saving Private Ryan*, however, it was a box-office failure in the United States. It could be argued that this is because it isn't patriotic, and that would be true; but it doesn't quite hit the mark. It isn't so much that *The Thin Red Line* is anti-patriotic, as that it operates at a different, deeper, more existential level altogether. Its concern is more metaphysics than politics; and it asks questions that undermine cosy, reassuring, this-worldly assumptions. It's far more profound, and therefore far more disturbing. And cinema audiences do not like to be *really* disturbed.

Whereas *Saving Private Ryan* is set in the early days of the Normandy landings in 1944, *The Thin Red Line* tells a story about the gruelling struggle of American troops to wrest the Pacific island of Guadalcanal from the Japanese in 1942. But it's not a conventional war story, because it uses the experience of war to raise deep questions about the nature of human existence and human destiny – or, to put it more precisely, it asks about the nature of human destiny, about what our prospects as human beings are, and therefore, in the light of that, it asks about the meaning of human existence.

So the focus of *The Thin Red Line* is not really the conventional one of the exploits of particular characters and their relationships; it is, rather, the solitary spiritual struggle of individuals, and the various ways in which different men respond to the extreme ambiguity of human existence – its bizarre combination of breath-taking beauty on the one hand and heart-stopping horror on the other.

At the film's core is an ongoing conversation – or, rather, a philosophical debate – between two characters, Sergeant Welsh and Private Witt. Welsh responds to the horror of war around him by trying to harden himself with cynicism. 'In this world', he tells Witt, 'a man is nothing. And there ain't no world but this one … We're living in a world that is blowing itself to hell as fast as everybody can arrange it. In a situation like this, all a man can do is shut his eyes and let nothing touch him – look out for himself.'

But Witt resists this option. He is captivated by the memory of the serenity with which his mother faced her own death – a serenity in which he believes he's seen 'the key to immortality'; and he refuses to permit the arbitrary horrors of war to eclipse the *equal* fact of profound beauty in the world – the beauty of nature, of good people, and of happy social life. 'You're wrong,' he says to Welsh. 'I've seen another world.'

This is really only the surface of his answer though; indeed, on most occasions Witt meets Welsh's cynical questions with silence. The real substance of his response is practical rather than verbal. His real answer is his refusal to harden himself, his persistence in caring for those around him, in gazing with compassion upon the agonized faces of comrades dying in his arms, in letting himself feel the pain, the awful tragedy, in remaining vulnerable.

In the end, Witt himself is killed as he deliberately draws the enemy away from a wounded soldier – 'Greater love hath no man' – and Welsh, later crouching at his graveside, asks, 'Where's your spark now?' In other words, Welsh is saying, 'What does the hope that enlightened you add up to now?' But everything hangs on the tone here. Is it the mocking voice of triumphant cynicism, '*Where's* your spark *now*?', or is it a genuinely open, quizzical, 'Where *is* your spark now?'

My own view is that it edges towards the latter; partly because Welsh, in spite of the all-too-evident cheapness of human life around him, just can't stop himself caring, and therefore can't stop himself yearning for something beyond mortality. The last words he speaks in the film, uttered in the privacy of his own soul, are these: 'If I never meet you in this life, let me feel the lack. A glance from your eye, and my life will be yours.'

Who is he speaking to? It can't be Witt himself, because Witt he certainly has met; it seems to be rather the Source of Witt's hope, the Original Fire of Witt's frail, but vital, spark. Sergeant Welsh is *praying*: 'If I never meet you in this life, let me at least feel the lack. A glance from your eye, and my life will be yours.'

One of the reasons that *The Thin Red Line* is such a persuasive, compelling film is that it offers no clean and easy resolution to the ambiguity of things. As Welsh puts it: 'One man looks at a dying bird, and thinks there's nothing but unanswered pain, that death's got the final word, laughing at him. 'Nother man sees the same bird, and feels the *glory*, feels something smiling through it.'

It seems to me, though, that the film does venture a statement, implicit but none the less definite. Or maybe it would be better to say that the film *shows us a sign*. The sign that it shows is the face of Witt: vulnerable, compassionate, gentle, but not at all weak, and most of all not afraid of death. A shining face. A face of arresting beauty; so beautiful, in fact, that to call it the face of a fool, would be, I think, an act of sacrilege. But if it's not the face of a fool, and it's not the face of an immortal, then what is it?

I think that the film presses us to see it as a *sign* of what it calls 'glory', but 'glory' here is not the same as in *Saving Private Ryan*. In the latter, the suffering and death of soldiers is justified, is given this-worldly meaning, by their service of the ideals of liberal democracy, which is represented at the beginning and end of the film by the wind-blown flag of the United States. One of its nicknames, of course, is 'Old Glory'.

The Thin Red Line, however, thinks that human suffering needs a 'glory' far bigger than that for its justification. Here, 'glory' clearly lies far beyond the nation and political ideology – however noble – and indeed beyond the world of time and space altogether. 'Glory' here speaks of that place where human life flourishes free from the secular ravages of war, betrayal and disease.

This glory does have its moments of presence in this world. *The Thin Red Line* opens on an island in the South Pacific in a village, where children gambol, where adults smile and laugh, and where the whole village sings hymns in perfect harmony. (And if we listen carefully, we notice that the music that accompanies this scene is, in fact, Gabriel Fauré's *In Paradisum*.)

Another is Private Bell's reveries of his beautiful young wife, of their love-making, and of her awaiting his return back home – reveries that sustain Bell as he risks his life in battle.

And then there's the shining face of Witt himself.

But all of these moments of 'glory' are shown by the film to be vulnerable, ephemeral, mortal: the village is struck down with strife and disease; Bell is stunned by a letter from his wife announcing that she's leaving him for another; and Witt, as I've mentioned, is killed.

So the question arises: are these moments of 'glory' merely illusions masking a basically brutal reality; or are they *signs* of a reality far deeper and more enduring than any of the brutal things that life can throw at us? What's more basic: the horror or the glory?

There are no certainties here, no proofs one way or the other, and *The Thin Red Line* is wise not to pretend that there are. But it nevertheless gives us a reason to bet on signs rather than illusions. What is this reason? It's the sheer, commanding beauty of the faces of those, like Private Witt, who trust and hope that the fragments of glory in this world – fragments of beauty, fragments of love, fragments of joy – are better clues to the origin and destiny of things than the forces of destruction.

Now whether we find this at all convincing will depend on whether we see beauty as mere decoration or as authority; but in favour of beauty as authority is the long philosophical tradition, beginning with Plato, that associates what's beautiful with what's true – a tradition reflected these days in the inclination of many natural scientists to take mathematical beauty as a measure of scientific truth.

So there's what *The Thin Red Line* has to say; and it seems to me that what it is saying is very close indeed to the heart of Christian faith. What it's saying, first of all, is that what's good in the world is more real, more basic, than what's brutal; what's good in the world is not an illusion, but a sign of the glory that lies on the far shores of suffering and death; and that therefore there is hope for those who suffer and die.

Second, *The Thin Red Line* says that there is a connection between hope and love – a two-way connection. On the one hand, *from hope to love*: in that those who are hopeful are prevented from the cynicism that hardens us and we are kept open for having care and compassion. It's not a coincidence that Private Witt, like Jesus, was both hopeful and compassionate.

On the other hand, there's also a movement *from love to hope*: in that those who dare to care for what is vulnerable and perishable (as all worthwhile things in this world are) find themselves compelled to hope, to yearn for the glory that surpasses this world. Even Sergeant Welsh, despite all his cynicism, can't help himself from praying: 'If I never meet you in this life, let me feel the lack ...'

The Thin Red Line can be summarized in a modified version of the words of St Paul in Romans 8:

Who shall separate us from the love of God that has been shown us in Jesus? Shall tribulation, or distress or persecution or famine or nakedness or peril or sword ... or gun or bomb or the warfare between our parents or the mockery of our peers or betrayal by our friends or professional failure or any other kind of injury that lacks redress here and now ...? No, in all these things we are more than conquerors through him who loved us. For I am sure that neither death, nor life; nor angels, nor principalities; nor things present, nor things to come; nor powers; nor height, nor depth; nor anything else in all creation, will be able to separate us from the love of God shining in the face of Jesus, who had faith, who had hope, who had compassion, who was raised from the dead, and whom we now follow.

The mustard seed and the yeast

Martyn Percy

Like a mustard seed, yeast is small. Moreover, it is lost and dispersed into the higher purposes to which it is given. And when Jesus talks about the kingdom of God as yeast – and our discipleship too – he is not advocating yeast for the sake of yeast. The notion of our discipleship is not that we are the yeast per se, but rather that we offer a yeast-like service to the world. It is about being the agent of transformation that is often small, or even unseen. It is about being immersed so deeply in the world and the parish that the depth of growth is often unquantifiable. As Einstein once said, that which truly counts in life can seldom be counted. The work of yeast is one of deep fission.

Baking bread offers us a rich analogy for what we are about. John Paul Lederach, in his book *The Moral Imagination: The Art and Soul of Building Peace*,[7] offers a rich meditation on our calling to be yeast. The most common ingredients for making bread are water, flour, salt, sugar and yeast. Of these, yeast is the smallest in quantity, but the one that makes the most substantial change to all the other ingredients. Lederach says you only need a few people to change a lot of things; one or two make all the difference to the millions. But yeast, to be useful, needs to move from its incubation and be mixed into the process – out of the seminary and into the parish, out of the Church and into the world. Both, like the proverbial manure, do the most good when they are spread around. And to some extent, week-by-week worship, even in the smallest congregation, is exactly what incubation is. We are preparing to go out to be catalysts for the kingdom – God's agents of change and transformation amid the mass of society. Yeast needs to be nurtured and thus grow.

Lederach tells a wonderful story of his early work in conciliation, when he was trying to build peace and consensus between the Yatama people and the Sandanista government. The work was risky and very dangerous, and Lederach had tried various strategies of direct facilitation, but without much success. Many of the meetings took place in Lederach's own house, and one day the warring chiefs asked him to leave so that the two sides could exchange quite frank and sharp views.

Lederach left – in a slight huff, it has to be said – and went into town to buy parts for his pick-up truck. But he had neglected to tell his wife who, back from shopping with their three-year-old daughter, found the house filled with about 15 heavily armed men, most of whom had a history of extreme violence. 'Who are you?' asked the men. 'I am Wendy,' she said, 'and I live here.' 'Oh,' they replied, 'come in – we are having a meeting.' Faced with the group she then surveyed, she simply said, 'Can I fix you guys some lunch?' They thanked her, and ate their fill.

Lederach goes on to say that what happened that day was *the* breakthrough in the Yatama–Sandanista negotiations. And it was because he had the courage – begrudgingly, granted – to get out of the way. He had provided a safe house, good hospitality and a secure process. And that was enough. In the end, the warring factions did not need or want him to be at the centre of what they were trying to do. He had been the catalyst, but he was not the result. He was their yeast. Or, rather, his wife was – the real agent of transformation in a challenging mix.

Sometimes we need small, dynamic agents of change. It just takes a few to do a lot. And sometimes the simplest things go a long way. Small things matter. The mustard seed is minute. But what is planted can, in the end, play host to so much and so many; the mustard seed reminds us that God can do some very promising things with the apparently negligible. So we have no mandate to try and divide the ingredients that God has given us and put them back in the cupboard. We are, rather, to add life and leaven to the mix, and we need to get on with the business of being God's yeast: getting stuck into the mix; being kneaded in. It is in giving that we receive; in dying that we are born to eternal life.

The art of building peace lies in blending together the disparate ingredients of the communities that we all serve. We can be the yeast that is kneaded in to make the bread; that we may all become one. But we need to find the courage to be God's catalyst, part of his deep work of change and growth.

To come together, in a simple act of worship, and to pray, be silent and recall, is in a real sense what God asks us to do, even in times of trauma, tribulation and senseless violence. But the prayer is, I think, that the yeast of the kingdom might still grow in us.

As Leslie Hunter (Bishop of Sheffield from 1939 to 1962) reminded us, there is always a risk when faith steps into a world of violence. But faith, hope and love is all we have – fragile though this seems – to help make any kind of new beginning. In some respects, his words apply as much now as they did during the darkest days of World War Two on which he reflects.

He argued that the tiny agents of change – the yeast and catalysts that could be you and me – are all God has to bring about change. Writing in *The Seed and the Fruit*,[8] Hunter offers this parable:

> As the threats of war and the cries of the dispossessed were sounding in our ears, humanity fell into an uneasy sleep. In our sleep we dreamed that we entered the spacious store in which the gifts of God to humanity are kept, and addressed the angel behind the counter, saying: 'We have run out of the fruits of the Spirit. Can you restock us?' When the angel seemed about to say 'no', we burst out: 'In place of violence, terrorism, war, afflictions and injustice, lying and lust, we need love, joy, peace, integrity, discipline. Without these we shall all be lost.' And then the angel behind the counter replied, 'We do not stock fruits here. Only seeds.'[9]

On judgement, repentance and restoration

Nigel Biggar

Wednesday is decision-day for me. Whenever I'm due to preach on a Sunday, I read the appointed lessons on the Monday before, mull them over on the Tuesday, and then decide what I'm going to preach about on the Wednesday. So, being decision-day, one particular Wednesday I had decided to run with what Providence had given me. What I had to offer were two loosely related Lenten fragments: reflections about repentance and judgement in the light of Jeremiah 18.1–11.

The context of this passage is that God's people stand under threat of invasion by the Babylonian empire. Perceiving this threat to be the judgement of God upon his people's wayward-ness, Jeremiah finds himself moved to say so in public. That is, he finds himself moved to become a prophet, declaring God's word of judgement. As is often the case, Jeremiah isn't entirely happy to assume the prophetic role. Like Moses before him, he protests his inadequacy. 'Ah, Lord GOD' he says, 'I do not know how to speak, for I am only a boy' (Jeremiah 1.6). But the word of God will not let him go, and it constrains him to speak.

True prophets are ones who don't much enjoy playing prophet. They don't enjoy alienating people, as speakers of uncomfortable truths tend to do. They don't enjoy the sound of their own soli-tary righteousness and they don't enjoy being in a minority of one. True prophets tend to find the whole business irksome and painful. They want to wriggle out of it, and they only take to the role with reluctance. So we need to be wary of those who take to prophecy like a duck to water; those who revel in the role. They probably aren't the real thing.

Back to Jeremiah though. By the time we reach him in chapter 18, it's the eleventh hour and the barbarians are at the gates. So he issues a very dramatic, graphic warning. Observing a potter, who summarily discards flawed products, Jeremiah warns the people of Judah that, unless they repent, God will treat them in the same way:

At one moment I may declare concerning a nation or a kingdom, that I will pluck up and break down and destroy it, but if that nation, concerning which I have spoken, turns from its evil, I will change my mind about the disaster that I intended to bring on it. And at another moment I may declare concerning a nation or a kingdom that I will build and plant it. (Jeremiah 18.7–10)

'If that nation ... And at another moment ... a nation'. There is a tone of breezy nonchalance in these words. Judah, God's self-styled 'chosen people', are accorded no privilege here: they are merely *a* nation whom God happens to have chosen; and what he has chosen he can easily *un*choose – according to their behaviour.

God will always have *a* people, but the people he has will be those who don't regard *his* favour as *their* property. A second thought is this: we Christians consider that, in a certain sense, the mantle of God's chosen peoplehood has moved on to our shoulders, so we are now the ones who stand in danger of religious presumption – of presuming upon his favour. But one thing we could do each Lent is to consider what might be the symptoms of presuming upon his favour, and whether they can be found among us.

In Jeremiah 18.12 we find Jeremiah predicting that Judah will ignore his warning: 'But they say, "It is no use! We will follow our own plans, and each of us will act according to the stubbornness of our evil will."' And in the following chapter we read that Jeremiah bought an earthenware jar from a potter, took himself into the presence of the elders of the people and their priests, deliberately smashed the jug in front of them, and announced that God will destroy Judah. Shortly afterwards, the Babylonians besieged Jerusalem, sacked it, and carried its people off into exile.

Clearly, it's not true that *every* calamity that befalls us is a judgement of God. Jesus himself made it clear that the disaster that befell the 18 who died when the tower in Siloam fell on them was not a punishment for some particular sin (Luke 13.1–5). Nevertheless, sometimes we do bring disaster on ourselves through doing what we ought not to do, or failing to do what we should. And sometimes, disaster is the *only* way to shake us out of complacency; the *only* way to get us to see the consequences of our actions; the *only* way to provoke repentance. It's tragic but it's true – sometimes disaster is the only route to salvation.

When I read about Jeremiah, and about the deep pain it caused him to foresee the dreadful destruction of his own people – of his own world – I am reminded of my hero, Helmuth James von Moltke. Von Moltke was an opponent of the Nazi regime during World War Two, who organized an ecumenical circle of leaders to plan for the reconstruction of Germany after the fall of Hitler. His life and witness are often commemorated on 23 January, the anniversary of his hanging in 1945.

Unlike Dietrich Bonhoeffer, von Moltke did *not* support von Stauffenberg's plot to blow up Hitler because he didn't want the Nazis replaced with a conservative regime dominated by a military aristocracy that would then negotiate peace. He believed that Germany had to suffer an unequivocal and catastrophic defeat, leaving not a single stone standing, so that it could be completely rebuilt from the bottom up. What a terrible, terrible thing for a patriot to wish for, and no doubt there were times when von Moltke, like Jeremiah at the end of chapter 20, rued the very day he'd been born. As Jeremiah cried, 'Cursed be the day on which I was born! The day when my mother bore me, let it not be blessed! … Why did I come forth from the womb to see toil and sorrow, and spend my days in shame?' (Jeremiah 20.14, 18).

Discussion of national sin, looming disaster, and the need for repentance brings to mind another thought. During the two hundredth anniversary of the abolition of the slave trade, there were calls for the British government to apologize for its past involvement in slavery. At the time I had thought, 'Well, we have: we abolished it – first, the trade in 1807 and then the institution in 1833.'

But we actually did much more than that. For over a century, from 1807 to 1914, the Royal Navy mounted anti-slavery patrols in the Atlantic and Indian Oceans. These patrols certainly didn't profit the Treasury, and they cost the Navy the lives of 17,000 sailors and marines. So not only did Britain repent of slavery, but through the Royal Navy's suppression of the slave trade, it did 100 years' worth of penance.

But here's a final thought. Britain's penance was certainly good for the British, in that it formed us into a more humane society, one for whom slavery is now generally abhorrent. And it was also good for the many Africans who would have been enslaved had the trade been allowed to thrive. It couldn't, though, undo the terrible injustice meted out to the millions who were robbed of their freedom, and who either died at sea in horrendous conditions or who survived to suffer the inhumanity of slavery.

That is the thing about human repentance and penance, especially in the case of grave wrongs: often they can't reverse the past – they can't undo what's been done. Trust remains damaged; the murdered remain in their graves. So human penance or compensation alone are often insufficient to lift the burden of guilt.

What's also needed is faith in God; a faith in a more-than-human power to make possible in the next life what is not possible in this one, faith in an almighty power to raise the innocent dead – in other words, our need for God's resurrecting power.

Litter: a moral and spiritual problem

Nigel Biggar

What makes litter a problem worthy of special attention? Surely there are far more pressing current issues to address: the capping of welfare receipts, say, the reform of banking regulation, or the rights and wrongs of a preventative strike against countries that we feel are a threat to us. Of course, there are social and environmental challenges far graver than littering, so what is the problem?

According to a 2009 report by Policy Exchange and the Council for the Protection of Rural England, litter dropped in the United Kingdom has increased by 500 per cent since the 1960s. We spend £500,000,000 every year in picking *some* of it up, mainly in urban areas. In the countryside, especially on the verges of rural roads, litter doesn't get picked up at all. It just lies there and accumulates, year after year.

Another problem with litter is rats, carriers of pathogens that can result in human disease. While the main cause of the increasing rat population is reckoned to be wetter weather, a subsidiary cause commonly mentioned is fast-food litter.

A third problem is an increase in antisocial behaviour. It is said that areas that *look* abandoned scare off law-abiding citizens and attract the not-so-law-abiding. And one of the earliest and most obvious symptoms of abandonment is accumulated litter.

Wasted money, more disease-carrying rats, and an encouragement to crime: these are three material, measurable problems that litter either causes or exacerbates, and which any utilitarian should be able to recognize.

But these things are not really what bothers me. They seem to be but the surface of two deeper problems: namely, trashing the beautiful and denying the public. This isn't just a precious, bourgeois illusion – not according to one newspaper story about women in a deprived inner-city neighbourhood complaining about the depressing unsightliness of litter blowing about in the streets.

So dropping litter in beautiful cities, or along rural roads, is a failure to respect what deserves respect, a slap in the face of beauty, and an intrinsic moral evil. It is a denial of personal responsibility, for all too often litter is seen as – someone *else*'s problem.

I have a sense that many of us have a *passive* attitude to what we share in common, and it doesn't do us any credit.

Littering doesn't have to be an inevitable feature of modern life – the French, Germans and Americans have a cleaner record. But the writer and retired prison doctor Theodore Dalrymple says the British habit of littering is not going to disappear any time soon, because it has tenacious social roots. Litter is a symptom of habitual unrestrained impulses learned in childhood.

So our individual efforts to combat litter are not likely to solve the problem in the short term, but they *can* alleviate it. Picking up litter is not just important because it helps to reduce the effects of the problem – it's also important because of what it says. It says, 'The public is mine; and I will care for it.' And by implication it says to others, 'The public is yours, and you should care for it too.' Picking up litter is a form of witness to a moral truth.

But why so much emphasis on litter in a Christian context? The answer is very simple. One of the most basic moral effects of believing and worshipping *one* God who creates and sustains *all things* in love is to raise our heads out of our private preoccupations to care for the wider world.

In 1 John 4.20 it says, 'Those who say, "I love God", and hates their brothers or sisters, are liars.' What this implies is that one cannot love God without at the same time loving the wider world that God loves. That's the theory, and there is hard empirical evidence that it works in practice. We Christians should lift our heads up out of our private, consumerist navels.

So we need to spend some time and energy on *un*trashing what's beautiful, and affirming what is public, by picking up litter in our surroundings. Because, if we claim to be Christians, we have to show we care.

In praise of moderation
Martyn Percy

> He also said, 'The kingdom of God is as if someone would scatter seed on the ground, and would sleep and rise night and day, and the seed would sprout and grow, he does not know how. The earth produces of itself, first the stalk, then the head, then the full grain in the head. But when the grain is ripe, at once he goes in with his sickle, because the harvest has come.' (Mark 4.26–29)

There is a lot of talk of unity these days, of our nations coming together. Unity is, it seems, flavour of the moment: united we stand, apparently. So I wrote this on the day that Donald J. Trump was inaugurated as the forty-fifth American President. Within hours of this happening, all mention of climate change had been redacted from the White House web pages. A new earth had arrived. New seeds had been planted.

In 2016 the *Oxford English Dictionary* named 'post-truth' as its Word of the Year. The term refers to statements that are manifestly untrue, but achieve the desired goal of persuading people to think or act differently. Specifically, it is defined as: 'relating to or denoting circumstances in which the objective facts are less influential in shaping public opinion than appeals to emotion and personal belief'.

So it is reasonable to peddle conspiracy theories for effect, even if the utterer does not believe one word of what is behind the theory. The use of language is designed to move, motivate and emotionally manoeuvre audiences. It is not about fact, but rather effect.

The question of truth – or what is now referred to as 'post-truth-politics' – is a defining question of our age. Politicians have always been economical with the truth, but post-truth politics is arguably new, and we now have a tide of rhetoric pandering to racism, misogyny, nativism, and a fear of immigrants who follow other faiths.

So does the Church's Week of Prayer for Christian Unity have anything to say to this? I think it does, for Christians have been quietly and determinedly working away for unity for several decades now. We don't accept our divisions as normal or desired; we work and pray for them to be overcome.

Yet in all of this we should perhaps remember that society and politics shape religion, as much as religion shapes the life of society. In 1952 the American pastor Norman Vincent Peale wrote the best-selling *The Power of Positive Thinking*,[10] which so manifestly has shaped the world of many in American politics. Peale's book launched the motivational thinkers' industry, and it has also shaped numerous Christian evangelical and fundamentalist ministries, built on the pillars of confidence, pragmatism, expectations of exponential growth and realizing our dreams, ambitions or visions. *The Power of Positive Thinking* shaped the church growth movement, health, wealth and prosperity movements, and many other expressions of capitalist-friendly fundamentalism. The hypothesis was simple enough: if you believe it enough, and keep saying it enough, it will be so. Your mind and its language, if fully positive, will ultimately reify your goal.

To some this might seem normal – an opportunity, even. American church-going embraced the free-market long ago. The rejection of any religious establishment opened the way for competition between individual churches and then produced the extraordinary organizational and theological creativity that distinguished the United States from all previous Christian societies. The price of this exuberance was doctrinal incoherence. In other words, if there is a bespoke Christian faith for everyone, the faith will mean almost anything – and therefore almost nothing. And this has effects that ripple out far beyond believers. A religion that is responsive to the pressures of the market becomes profoundly fractured, and in the end a market-driven religion gives rise to a market-driven approach to truth. There were churches on both sides of the civil war in the United States; and churches on both sides of the civil rights struggle. As Martin Luther King observed, the United States is never more segregated than on a Sunday morning.

So, what of Christian unity? Specifically in Anglican terms, it is perhaps worth pointing out that Anglican polity is first and foremost a social vision that has ecclesial consequences. It is not an ecclesial polity with accidental social consequences. The Elizabethan Religious Settlement of 1559 was a social vision for breadth, inclusiveness, charity, generosity and diversity – it produced the *Prayer Book*. The *Prayer Book* did not produce that society. The *Prayer Book* is not the cause of the Settlement: it is just one result of that Settlement.

Settlement is a tiny seed, to be sure. But Anglicanism is not alone in being a social vision first, and a church second. We can think of Methodists, and in particular a word used of their polity in governance: 'moderator'. It is not the only church to be governed by a moderator, but the word implies that 'moderation' – the practice and virtue of being intentionally and dispositionally 'moderate' – might be incredibly important for social and ecclesial life.

The word was originally used of weather and other physical conditions. But the one who moderates is the one who works within peaceable bounds, and practises restraint. The moderator 'regulates, mitigates, restrains, tempers …' – one who 'abates excessiveness' and gently but firmly 'presides' over 'potentially divisive debates'. In his book *Faces of Moderation: The Art of Balance in an Age of Extremes*,[11] Aurelian Crăiuţu argues that moderation is not an ideology, but rather a disposition. It is a composite of character and virtues that does not divide the world into light and dark, true and false, good or bad. At the same time, moderation does not accept everything as equal and valid. It does not, for example, split the difference between racism and inclusion. It accepts that some opinions and ideologies are irredeemable, and should be rejected. Rather, moderation works at unity and harmony. And it accepts that on our own, we cannot be entirely right or good. We need one another, and we need to value and cherish our differences – and sometimes our disagreements – if we are to progress.

In an earlier book,[12] Crăiuţu argued that moderation was a virtue for courageous minds. Tacitus mourned the lost virtue of moderation – calling moderation 'the most difficult lesson of wisdom'. Being a moderate, a bit like being ecumenical, is not weak-willed or sloppily liberal: it is about being charitable, generous and tough-minded. In other words, it is a difficult blend. But this is the calling of all denominations in the Week of Prayer for Christian Unity: to live as generous moderators.

We live in uncertain times – an age of austerity, anxiety, assertion and anger. It can all feel a bit unstable, but institutions such as universities, galleries, museums – and, most especially, our churches – are called to be stable, public bodies that transcend such times. They are places of inclusive learning and profound reflection; they are here for human and social flourishing, nourishing and learning. These places are called to be oases of moral agency and social capital. We are here to create citizens and cultivate citizenship, and build civilization.

That is why I am so committed to the mild, temperate and middle ground so beloved of Anglican polity, and to the virtue of moderation. I believe that to be honed in the manner of Christ is to become 'gentle, meek and mild'; and if we can create a mild cultural climate, we will discover that freedom flourishes in temperate zones. It does not survive the burning faith of demagogues, prophets and crowds, as Raymond Aron once remarked. But we know too, as Isaiah Berlin said, that the middle ground is a notoriously exposed place; a dangerous and difficult position to inhabit. However, it is the place for government. As the philosopher Michael Oakeshott once opined, the business of government is not to inflame passion and give it new subjects to feed off, but to inject into the activities of already too passionate people an ingredient of moderation.

We are taught that perfect love casts out fear; but perfect fear can cast out love. Inclusivity was, and is, a deep *value* rooted in nothing less than the gospel. Inclusivity is on the heart of God. It drives the vision of the early Church: a place where there is neither Jew nor gentile, slave nor free, male or female – but all are one in Jesus Christ.

Moderation may seem like a tiny seed, and in some ways it is. So in the Week of Prayer for Christian Unity, we do well to remember that what Jesus inaugurated was eternal: 'the just and gentle rule of the kingdom of God' – inclusive, prophetic, pastoral, kind, wise and foolish. And to live and practise this most taxing of blends, we need to become seeds of moderation, and God's most generous moderators, to settle and establish his kingdom.

The Week of Prayer for Christian Unity incites us to be a people of fervent faith and calm temperament; a people of moderation and passionate commitment; and we are invited to be agents of its inauguration.

Everybody wants a happy ending
(Reflections on Ian McEwan's *Atonement*)
Nigel Biggar

If you haven't read Ian McEwan's *Atonement*[13] or seen the film of the novel, and don't want the ending spoiled, don't read on – otherwise all will be revealed very shortly. But if it's any consolation, I do think that the story is worth reading or the film viewing, even when you know what's coming, because the issues that it raises bear reflecting on.

Here's the story in a nutshell.

Briony, the not-quite-adolescent daughter of an English country household in the 1930s, is a budding writer who enjoys the god-like power of ordering fantasy worlds – and ordering the world according to her fantasy.

Impelled by an over-active imagination, she gets it into her head that Robbie, the friend of her elder sister, Cecilia, is a sex maniac. Then one night her cousin Lola is raped, and Briony assumes that Robbie did it. He didn't, but Briony swears that she saw him. Robbie is arrested, convicted and sent to prison, his would-be medical career aborted. War then breaks out. Robbie is drafted into the army, shipped to France, slightly wounded, and eventually finds himself stranded on the beaches of Dunkirk, awaiting evacuation.

Will Robbie be reunited with Cecilia? Will Briony be reconciled with her sister, now estranged, and with Robbie? Will there be atonement? Will there be a happy ending?

Meanwhile, back in England, Briony has become a nurse, doing hard penance by caring for the wounded, mutilated and dying young men recovered from Dunkirk – and, in her spare time, trying to order the fateful past by writing a novella about it.

Eventually, she tracks Cecilia down in her flat and discovers Robbie there, just returned from France. The encounter is tense; and Robbie is only just restrained from violence. But it ends with Briony promising to make public confession of her perjury, with a view to securing Robbie's pardon. Atonement is just around the corner.

Fast forward from 1940 to 1999. Briony, now an accomplished writer, is dying; and she is reflecting on her last novel, which will be published posthumously. It is in fact the final version of the novella that she had begun as a nurse, but had not been able to complete over the intervening 59 years. The reason that she'd not been able to complete it was that the whole truth was, in fact, unbearable to her.

The truth is that she never did meet Cecilia and Robbie again in 1940. That ending, which was at least open to the possibility of final happiness, had been merely her literary fabrication – a figment of her ordering imagination. In fact, Robbie had died of blood-poisoning at Dunkirk, and Cecilia had been killed in the Blitz. Briony had not confessed her perjury, because it could have achieved nothing. Atonement had been put beyond the reach of possibility.

In the last three intriguing pages of the book, McEwan has Briony muse on why it was that she had pulled her literary punch – why she'd not been able to bring herself to give the story its true, pitiless conclusion:

'How could that constitute an ending?' she says. 'What sense or hope or satisfaction could a reader draw from such an account? Who would want to believe that they never met again, never fulfilled their love? Who would want to believe that, except in the service of the bleakest realism? I couldn't do it to them … I no longer possess the courage of my pessimism …'

The problem of these 59 years has been this: how can a novelist achieve atonement when, with her absolute power of deciding outcomes, she is also God? There is no one, no entity or higher form that she can appeal to, or be reconciled with, or that can forgive her. There is nothing outside her.

Briony writes as an atheist and, I suspect, McEwan writes as an atheist through her. So if there is nothing beyond, no God and no afterlife to which God can bring us, then there is no atonement for the likes of Briony, Robbie and Cecilia. There is no healing. Just the wound, left forever gaping.

But I think it's remarkable that Briony cannot muster the courage of her pessimism, and it's even more remarkable that nor can McEwan. In the very last lines of his book, he has Briony say this:

> I like to think that it isn't weakness or evasion, but a final act of kindness, a stand against oblivion and despair, to let my lovers live and to unite them at the end. I gave them happiness, but I was not so self-serving as to let them forgive me. Not quite, *not yet*. If I had the power to conjure them … Robbie and Cecilia, still alive, still in love … *It's not impossible*.
> But now I must sleep.[14]

What does she mean, 'Not yet', and 'It's not impossible'?

According to atheism, the whole truth is that there is no 'not yet'; and it is entirely impossible. Since there is nothing outside us, since there is no Beyond, atonement is nowhere on the horizon. So what does McEwan mean by ending his book on an ambiguous, tentatively hopeful note?

And, of course, the film of his book is far less tentative, leaving us in its concluding scene with Robbie and Cecilia, very much alive and very much in love beneath those wartime icons of home-coming and safety, the White Cliffs of Dover.

From an atheist's point of view, this is all so much loss of nerve, so much failure of courage in the face of pitiless truth. These stands against oblivion and despair can be nothing other than absurd, even contemptible moments of weakness.

From a Christian's point of view, on the other hand, these stands against despair, these shy assertions of hope and possibility, are reflex expressions of faith. Faith that what is evidently *not* possible in this world, within the bounds of time and space, is *yet* possible – possible beyond, beyond this world, beyond the power of any human art.

And it's remarkable that atheists such as Briony, and her own literary creator, just can't seem to stop themselves affirming what they claim to be absurd. Is it really just weakness? Or might the visceral revolt against ultimate injustice be an expression of inadvertent wisdom?

Now, of course, wanting something to be true doesn't make it so. Badly wanting a happy ending – badly wanting ultimate atonement – doesn't give us the right to believe in it. Strength of will or desire or need doesn't amount to a ground or reason. It was the German social theorist Max Horkheimer who once said that just because it's too awful to suppose that generations of innocents will never see justice, doesn't give us warrant to believe that God is coming to their rescue at the End of Time.

Well, that would appear to be true – and yet I wonder. I think it's missing something, but what it is missing is quite hard to articulate. But here are some thoughts.

There are two different kinds of wishful thinking. One is magical thinking that would make the world serve one's selfish purposes by force of will or imagination or ritual. This is childish, immature and egotistical; and what is wished for is usually trivial.

But the kind of wishful thinking that Briony and McEwan can't stop themselves from, the kind of wishful thinking that is faith, is altogether more serious, more grave, more weighty – and it's born not of childish selfishness, but of a very grown-up *love* for people and their flourishing.

The hope for the raising up of human beings beyond death, the hope for ultimate healing and atonement, is born of love for things that are intrinsically valuable. It's as if their injury and rupture and death naturally appears to us as a sacrilege, as a deep wrong that must be righted – if not here and now, then there and then.

The desire, the hope for the resurrection of the dead, and the binding of what's been ruptured is an extension, it seems to me, of the logic of love. It's not merely that death and ultimate rupture aren't *wanted*. It's more that they *just don't make sense*. It is *they* that are absurd.

Loving the goodness and beauty of human fulfilment makes sense. Loving what deserves love makes sense. And continuing to love them even when death has taken them beyond our care, makes better sense than concluding that our love was foolish.

The yearning for a happy ending and the refusal of ultimate pitilessness – whether it be Briony's or McEwan's – is not an absurd failure of courage. It's a natural expression of love, impelled by the intrinsic value of what love embraces to assert religious faith in the face of all that death cuts absurdly short.

Love might be mistaken, of course. The world might be so designed as to cause love to lead us by the nose into hope, only to have death make fools of us. It could be so. Only the End of Time will tell.

In the meantime, it is not at all clear to me that the ultimate pitilessness of things makes more sense than the logic of love and its natural extension into religious faith. And I draw strength from the fact that, when push comes to shove, it's not even clear to atheists like Ian McEwan.

Healing the centurion's servant

Martyn Percy

I suppose the first thing to ask is, 'What was the purpose of Jesus' healing miracles?' After all, he healed lots of people. But not everyone, of course. So if the miracles are 'signs', what did they point to? Because that is what signs do – they point and inform. Part of the answer has to lie in locating the healing ministry of Jesus within the activity of the incarnation which, in some sense, is an ongoing process. In the incarnation, that which is symbolized in Christ is also actualized, and the hidden revealed: the Church is called to live out this life too, relating the inner to the outer in all spheres.

So the miracles of Jesus are real in the sense that all symbolic action became focused on activity that was observable and demonstrable. This apparently involves disturbing the laws of nature, but the laws are only subverted where they oppress or threaten, and Jesus' healing activity points to the importance of breaking through all oppressive barriers, be they legal, societal or 'natural'. Again, this suggests that miracles can never be 'proofs' or simple demonstrations of 'power': they always have a social-transcendent function that is primary.

The social, moral, religious and political impacts of Jesus' healing miracles are inescapable. Part of the value of these miracles in Jesus' ministry, apart from healing individuals, seems to be in questioning society over its attitude to illness itself. The sin of the individual as a cause is uniformly rejected by Jesus. Instead, he tends to challenge crowds and onlookers, questioning their implicit or explicit role in the person's misfortune. For Jesus, healing is never just an action for an individual: there are always wider, corporate implications.

So what should we make of the healing of the centurion's servant in the Gospels of Matthew and Luke? I think we should note some obvious things, either implied or embedded in the text, that are perhaps at first sight *not* obvious. First, the centurion is not a Jew. The text would tell us if he were. He is almost certainly a foreigner, and therefore a person of another faith – or perhaps none – but I think it's more likely to be a person who follows another religion. Second, the same is likely to be true of the servant or slave. Luke tells us he is 'valuable' to the centurion – so he is almost certainly a foreigner purchased in one of the many slave markets. Like the centurion, the servant is not a Jew, but someone of another faith, or none. Third, the Jews who petition Jesus either forget this, or don't seem to mind. Because they simply say that this centurion – despite being non-Jewish and of another faith – has none the less helped them build their synagogue. So the centurion is valuable to the Jews.

Jesus helps the centurion, and heals the servant. Neither becomes a good Jew – or a Christian – as a result of this. So yes, the love of God in Jesus extends to people of other races, other tribes, and other faiths – again, without conditions. The love of God, poured out in Jesus, is beyond tribal, national, ethnic and religious backgrounds. Jesus gives us a sign. It points the way.

The story of the centurion and his servant and the whole story of Elijah (a prophet who struggled with Arabs and other foreigners and, much to his indignation, was helped and enabled by both) both have some important things to say about foreigners, and how we belong to one another.

The Jews when they looked at the centurion did not see a foreigner, but someone who had helped them construct something with them and for them – a synagogue. The alien was now 'one of us', and so they beseech Jesus to help the man, and his servant. It is typical of Jesus to heal people outside the margins of the chosen, privileged and tribal. Jesus is an integrationist; his vision for the kingdom of God is integrationist too. Most countries take pride in their 'national character', but this can easily become insularism – born of a deep anxiety about being part of something larger. Such anxiety is not about being alone or isolated. Paradoxically, it is about *togetherness* and equality: being blended in with others. In Matthew and Luke the centurion is an external, foreign agent who has helped the Jews to become even better Jews – because he helped them build their synagogue. This group of Jews did not turn away the alien and stranger. They accepted the benefits of their integration, even though they may not have originally wished for it.

When Jesus heals a person, he also touches the social context and culture that frames the disorder and disease. He hears the dumb; he speaks to the deaf; he sees the blind; and he touches the untouchable. The body of Christ is richly sensate. It also reaches outside itself, and incorporates others.

Touching is one of the most basic forms of human communication, and one of the most personally experienced of all sensations. Our tactile sense is the genesis of our individual and social awareness. Closeness and physical intimacy play a major part in addressing pain: a hand extended in friendship or consolation, a hug or embrace can be more profound than a thousand words. Neighbours mattered to Jesus. He talked about Good Samaritans. He praised a Syrophonecian woman's faith. He heals the foreign servant of a foreign centurion. In all these instances, we are being invited to contemplate our mutual belonging.

The remarkable story of Jesus' healings is his awareness of this dynamic: he was willing to touch and be touched – he expressed grace in his physicality. Individually and socially, the Church needs to contemplate real touching in response to real alienation and pain. This engagement requires a deep reaching inside itself, as well as a reaching out, drawing on the resources of the one whose incarnation is just that. And if the Church wants to retrieve the healing miracles of Jesus, it can't adopt this stance. It will have to engage with the more subversive political motivations that lie behind Jesus' healings and his stand on integrationism.

You might think that Brexit and Grexit are new problems. But let me relate a story about Oxfam. It celebrated its 75th birthday in 2017, and it begins with Greek debt, European tensions, wars, too many refugees and asylum seekers in Europe, and not enough to go around. Oxfam was started in 1942 by some House men and others in Oxford who were concerned about famine in Greece as a result of the allied blockade.

Of course, you could not get food in Greece. People responded with odd gifts – butter, jewellery, etc.; and a warehouse in Broad Street was opened to store it. But the manager of the warehouse realized you couldn't send butter to Greece, or even jewellery. So he hit upon the idea of selling it to locals – and sending the money as aid to Greece.

That shop opened some 75 years ago, and it is literally the mother of all charity shops. But the source of all this? It is goodness and openness – and a spirit of true internationalism. But the traffic is not all one-way. The Gospels teach us that we are not better off on our own. We are better off when we look after our neighbours – and we perhaps might realize they also look after us.

But who would have bet on a group of Jews petitioning Jesus to heal a centurion's slave? And Jesus would later tell a story about the Good Samaritan too – another nearby foreign neighbour who helped a Judean who would rather have been self-sufficient, and left alone. The Church isn't about that. It is about figuring out how we benefit, mutually, from being together.

Story

The Pigs Can Swim

MARTYN PERCY

I live on my own these days. No one inside me, and no one beside me. Free as a bird.

I am glad I left them. They would have thrown me out anyway. They always did. Even as a child – when I thrashed around with all the piercing, raucous voices inside my head, and the tongues pouring out of my throat, not sounding like me at all, but like some sick intonation from that abyss of darkness, filth and evil – they shut me out. They say I was born spouting obscenities, profanities and blasphemies. Oh, they tried to silence me, I know. God knows they tried.

The doctors came in their droves. They weighed my stools, took my pulse, felt my fevered head. I just shook violently. They shook their heads. You could see the fear in their eyes; and the doubts. The anxious looks to my brothers and sisters, who were always shooed away. Those helpless glances made at my father and mother. But my parents were not looking my way at all. They never were. They stood gazing into the distance, or looking up, despairing at the aching void of sky. Like they were forsaken.

I was a void too. A big empty cave, full of rabid bats, straight from the bowels of hell. They screamed at each other in the night, and every time I opened my mouth they spat themselves out. They disgusted me. But I was their host.

The quacks came too, with their potions. They were a joke. Some oil here, a cream there. A magic pill. A new diet. Perhaps I was allergic to something I was eating? Would a massage help, perhaps? Some soothing aromatherapy to calm my troubled soul? Give me a break. Inside, the voices raged. One of these quacks was such a bleeding charlatan I just lunged for him, and decked him. Caught him square on the jaw with a mighty great thump. Peach of a punch, it was. We never saw him again.

The therapists came too with all their bloody enquiry and tiresome empathy. All those rhetorical questions. 'You seem to have a lot of anger?' they'd say. Or, 'You seem to be having difficulties relating to your parents.' Too damn right. My parents kept me locked in the shed at the bottom of the olive grove, tied to the water pump with a chain around my foot, while I shouted and screamed all night. I scratched that shed door like a caged cat, until my fingernails bled.

I won't deny I foamed and frothed at the mouth with my legion tongues. And I couldn't renounce the voices in my head, not ever, and all the filth that poured off my lips. I ate my food off the floor in a bowl, like a rabid dog. But I had the strength of several men to break those restraints – to snap the chains. I once burrowed out of the shed using my teeth and hands. Getting out of those straightjackets was a piece of cake. I ripped the padded cells to shreds, and I ate half the stuffing.

Then there were the exorcists. God, they needed sorting. Two kinds, there were. One lot came in their pristine white three-piece suits, with their expensive watches. They jabbered away in their dreary southern drawl, then upped a gear or two to get into their intense breathy Pentecostal tongues. But I always had more tongue-babble than them, and mine was much louder. I screamed them out. They fled, shouting that the house was cursed. In truth, they were just beaten. 'Demons defeated!', they had claimed before they even started with their exorcisms. My arse; we won every bout. There was no contest.

Another lot came in pencil-thin black cassocks with their beards and beads, consulting their old leather liturgy books for litanies. Daft lot, they were. I just used to stare back, in total silence, with a vacant look in my eye. I said nothing. They sloped away, depressed.

Then they sent the technicians, with their batteries, wires and clamps. God knows what they did to me. I shook and convulsed like never before, and then finally slept, exhausted. For some while after the volts had surged through, I felt nothing. Nothing: like I was floating on a sheet of glass, on sheets of cool ice, somewhere in outer space. It was all dark blue and chilled. Nothing above, below or beside me. Just me. Bliss. Totally alone.

But it didn't last. It never did. The voices came back. More and more each time. Worse and worse, I passed out and felt emptied, only for more to climb in. I was full of them. So full I could not breathe. They seethed inside me, and they choked my breath. These voices fumed with rage. They fought each other for possession of my lungs, my head and my tongue. My speech became a boiling babble of noise. I was a fountain of filth. Rubbish spewing rubbish. A spouting sewer. A walking obscenity. Pure dirt.

So they threw me out. Not out of the house this time. Those days were long gone. I was grown up now, you see. And I could break the fetters. I could thump the doctor. I could lay out the therapist cold. A well-aimed punch was more than a match for any empathy. No one would treat me. No one came near. My parents were broke. It had cost them everything. The neighbours were disgusted. They tried to move away, but couldn't sell their houses. I had become a 'social problem', you see.

So my parents grieved to themselves, and told me I was dead. No longer their son. And they took me to the place of the dead. They chained me up in the graveyard outside the village, and they left me there. I still broke the chains. I would come back at night, and try and crawl into my own bed late at night for comfort. Sometimes I broke in. But eventually I was locked out for ever. They built new fences and walls, and changed the locks. They sold up and moved away. I never saw them again.

No matter, the village was still my home. But now the neighbours stood guard on the edge of the parish, like sentinels. They beat me back with clubs if I went anywhere near the place or the people. Many a time I went back to the graveyard, cursing and cut, bruised and battered. I foraged for food. I lived alone among our dead – my only friends. My only company.

Then he came. No idea who he was. But he had a group of friends who followed him, and I saw him in the distance. I did not dare go near. I thought I'd get clubbed. The sniping voices in me tormented me, and said, 'He is dangerous; he means to harm you; hide, quickly.' But the voices were nervous that day; I could tell. I tried to walk away and hide. But I couldn't. I froze.

All morning I watched him, sitting on his own. Then the herds-woman walked by with her pigs. She stopped, and started chatting to the stranger. No idea why. She usually kept herself to herself. I had often seen her with swine, weaving their way through the dry wadis and wilderness. Sometimes I'd wave, and she'd half-signal back – friendly-like, but wary too. But we never spoke; and we never came close to it. She had a favourite pig too – a piglet, really. It used to walk beside her like some kind of obedient puppy. The sight of it always made me laugh. Who the hell has a pet pig?

But today, they just stood there, the three of them – the stranger and this woman, and her pet pig – not so far from the cemetery where I now crouched in the shadows of the tombstones. His friends hovered in the distance, watching. And then the stranger, the woman and her pig just started walking towards the tombs. Towards me. He didn't say anything at first. He just waved at me from a distance. Stupidly, I waved back. God knows why.

The voices in my head squealed like a pig that was about to be butchered, and had just had its throat cut. 'Run, you moron' the voices said, 'Run'. It was one of the deepest, throaty voices of mine – but one now struggling for its own right to breathe.

But I couldn't move. I stood staring, rooted to the spot. And now I could see his face, and he was smiling at me. At me. No one smiled at me. Ever. I got fear and loathing in people's faces; or the back of their heads as they ran. But he smiled. It wasn't an ordinary smile. It was one of compassion, kindness and wisdom. I had never seen such a look, even in my parents' faces.

And the next thing I remember he was standing right next to me, patting the pig on the head, but looking at me with these deep brown eyes, with the herdswoman standing nearby. The pig just looked up at him, like it was a newly trained puppy and he was the master. He began to speak, and all I remember hearing was the voice.

It was one voice in my head, clear as a bell – and not the jangling many I hear all the time. And it was a deeper voice than anything I had heard before or since. Deeper than the abyss where my tongues came from, and higher than the sky when I blanked out. The voice seemed to sing, but I don't remember a word of it. No, not one. Just the sound.

Then it happened. I felt my stomach heave, my lungs explode, my guts erupt and my heart split. My legs gave way, and I doubled up in staggering pain – deeper than anything I had ever known. My mouth went dry, and my head began to scream inside – a thousand shrieking, screeching, squealing yells. They came from the pit of my guts, and I felt my insides swell – an almighty heave.

And I threw up. The vomit just surged out. The puke hurled through the air. Whole pitchers of the stuff, or so it seemed. Like bats screeching through the air. And as it all poured out, all I felt was this amazing calm, and this sudden rush of pure, clean air, all scented like some rosemary of the desert. I was empty.

I collapsed to the ground, and must have been out of it for a fair bit. But when I came to, I saw the stranger's face, and he was just smiling at me. There might even have been a chuckle. But then all I could see was the puke – all over the front of his robe. Dripping. Nasty, green foul-smelling, bilious retch. It stank. He saw me look at it, and then he looked down, and he just wiped it off with his hand. I felt this great wave of shame. But he didn't seem remotely disgusted. Not a bit of it.

He just offered his puke-sodden hand to the pig, who gave it a long lick, but no more than that. Pigs will eat anything, you know. But I don't reckon the pig liked the taste of my spew that much. So the stranger wiped the rest of the vomit on the pig's hairy haunch, and patted the pig on the head like a puppy dog. It was almost like the pig was being anointed.

Then it all kicked off. The pig went berserk – rabid, really. It ran round and round in circles trying to eat its tail; and then it tore off at a rate of knots like one of those bats out of hell inside me, ploughing straight into the rest of the herd, scattering them for just a moment. They squealed like they were about to all be slaughtered. For several moments, they all sounded like me – thousands of profanities and obscenities screeching from the herd. The herdswoman went running after them, but it was too late. The herd came back together in an instant, seemed to go totally bonkers, and tore off down the track on the hillside in a loopy sprint, towards the small cliff-edge by the lake. They never even tried to stop.

Now, pigs can't fly. We all know that. Even when I was at my maddest, I never saw a pig with wings. So I'll be the first to admit that the speed and impact with which they hit the water would concern anyone who was watching. But you see a pig is basically a hippo with hooves. Only smaller. Of course they can swim.

So I never understood what all those writers were talking about, years later, when they say the herd had all drowned. That the whole herd had to die because all pigs are unclean and defiling. That's all just rubbish. Pigs are lovely animals.

But what those pigs did that day was run like a bunch of demented dogs. They hurtled off the steep embankment, and plunged into the water, and then they all swam round and round, squealing at the top of their high-pitched piggy shrieking. Sounding just like me. Hundreds of them. But later, they all came ashore, safe and sound. They lay exhausted on the lakeside in the hot midday sun, and baked themselves dry.

I asked the stranger to take me with him. Wherever he was going, really. I'd follow him. But he wouldn't allow this. He told me to go home. Well, my folks had left the village long ago, and I knew their house was empty: cursed, the villagers said. But I did as I was told, and so walked back to the village at dusk that very same day.

It's madness, said the villagers, you being back. We're all civilized here now. You don't really belong. They threw stones at me, and boarded up their windows and double-locked their doors. There were some who were kinder, and a few greeted me distantly across the street. But most gave me a wide berth. They're bastards, the lot of them. They chained me up for years. And I can't forgive them for that. I can't trust them, you see. They say I'm mad, and I belong in an institution. But I'm finally free. It is them that are mad.

Years later, I thought of that one pig hurtling off like some kind of deranged scape-goat, covered in my legion spew. I thought of it wandering mad and alone in the wilderness. But like the scape-goats of old, it only went away for a short while, and once washed, then bleached in the searing sun, came back to its own. As right as rain, it was.

So I live on my own now, in my shed in the foothills. Sometimes

I wave at that herdswoman in the distance, with her new piglets and all the old pigs, and she half waves back. I never saw that stranger again. Never. True pigs can't fly, and I can only imagine their terror as they hurtled off a deep-sloped embankment. But they swim pretty well, you know. So I'm happy here in my hut, looking at the valleys below, watching the pigs paddling and playing in the shallows of the lake, oinking and snorting.

In the hot summer dusks, I sometimes sneak to the shore while the herdswoman takes her nap, and go swimming with the pigs. They go much deeper into the lake, where it is cooler. I love to see pigs swim. And there's still no one inside me and no one beside me. Just the odd pig for company. And I am as free as a bird.

Part 2

Sermons and Homilies for the Christian Year

Waiting in Advent

Graham Ward

There is something deeply pagan about Advent in the northern hemisphere as we move towards the winter solstice. Anyone who has experienced Advent in the Antipodes or in a Mediterranean country sees the coming of Christ quite differently. But the Near Eastern character of Christian origins gets lost at this time of the year when the Celtic fogs and the wildness of the weather, which Julius Caesar abhorred so much when he came to conquer Britain, steep us in darkness from late afternoon until early morning. Darkness protracts time. 'Is it only half-past five?' we say, the curtains having already been drawn much earlier – because the darkness seems to go so deep as the hours of daylight shorten. We go to work and return home in the dark. Of course, when the sky, even during the day, is gunmetal grey those of us who are not Californians or Australians feel light-deprived. Candles and fires take on a felt pertinence that central heating and fluorescent bulbs can't emulate. That's where the pagan gets evoked: bonfires and blood in a fight against darkness and cold.

Climate, latitude and the angle at which the Earth tilts as it orbits the sun have not only made life possible on this planet, they have shaped the futures of that life. We wouldn't be here as human beings if the climate had not changed to such an extent that we sought and devoured more and more meat, which expanded our brains and demanded we stood on two feet to move. When the

climate changes again – with or without our irresponsible assistance – there may well be rude awakenings that follow. We should
give thanks for the global openness towards rectifying the damage
we have done to the environment because otherwise we may well
return to the caves and rock shelters we left some 30,000 years
ago. Some people, out of present necessity, have never left them.
I'm not quite apocalyptic, but it doesn't take much brain-ache to
realize resources are not limitless and, for many, downright scarce
already. In northern climes, we dwell in darkness in a different
way than they dwelt in the time of Isaiah or even St Paul. We
dwell also in a different way than our grandfathers even – with
the sea levels rising and weather systems worsening.

The paganism and seasonal swings of the northern hemisphere
bring something profound to our experiences of Advent. They
colour our imaginations when we read Scripture; they lend a
certain tone – and even urgency – to our appreciation of a coming
light. They bring a brooding to our waiting. Isaiah recalls this
quality of waiting: 'we have waited for him, so that he might save
us ... we have waited; let us be glad and rejoice in his salvation'
(Isaiah 25.9). This quality of waiting has a local and seasonal
resonance. It takes on the embodiment of place. We wait longer
for the light in the northern hemisphere, where often the snow is
already deep by the season of Advent, and the isolation of winter
is already locking people into their houses. It is then that the waiting is even more pronounced. Time hangs in waiting; but while it
hangs a space is opened up for reflection and meditation. Part of
the difficulty with modern Christmases is that we become totally
preoccupied with the planning, preparation and work necessary
for the Christmas event itself: presents, cards, shopping for sup-
plies and food. The only time for reflection is when the shops
shut at five-thirty on Christmas Eve and all that can be bought
has been bought for the feasts to follow. In busy lives, we have
to learn to wait, but we have to set aside time for that waiting
to be possible. And even then we can be so preoccupied that the
space of waiting gets eaten up with thoughts about what is yet to
be done, and when it is going to be done. So Advent as a time of
discipline, and principally the discipline of experiencing what it is
to wait, gets a low priority. But without learning and practising

the art of waiting – and it is an art because it demands we craft our experience of how time hangs – then we miss something of what Advent is all about. The light has not yet come. We dwell in darkness. We have to bring to mind how deep that darkness goes and how lost we are within it, within ourselves.

Exhausted of inspiration we wait. We, like Isaiah, know what we are waiting for: salvation. We have waited for it for a lifetime. But we don't know what salvation looks like. In Psalm 37 we are told to delight in the Lord and he will give us the desires of our hearts – but we don't know what it is we desire. There are objects we can hook on to, just as we can draw up a Father Christmas list of what we think salvation should bring. Feasting and good wine, Isaiah tells us. But what are we really desiring in these things? Salvation is a name we give to the namelessness of our desire. We wait – assured for all our past dealings with God that we hope to recognize salvation when it comes. Waiting demands we open ourselves to a future of transformation and hope, but in the darkness, our pagan, northern hemisphere darkness, such openness makes us vulnerable. And we don't like vulnerability. We are an impatient species, and waiting demands we peer ahead into what we have to discern rather than see. Is this the dawn – or moonlit snow on distant hills? Is this an angel stirring wind-chimes with a message of arrival, or the stirring of ghosts of old loves that still haunt us? The light dawns, but will we know it has dawned, that this *is* the light? How many of us would have recognized Christ in and as a Jewish peasant? If Christ comes as a man begging a coat on a frosty night when the snow is deep and crisp and even, will we know him? Will we know that offering that coat will utterly transform us? We *have* waited, Isaiah tells us. We *have* waited. But how many of us *have* waited in this pagan darkness sparkling with Christmas card glitter and frantic tinselled activities? This year will I wait?

Two readings for Christmas: abiding

Martyn Percy

Abiding 1: God makes a home with us

Here is one of the better jokes pulled from a Christmas cracker last year. Good King Wenceslas rings up his local pizzeria. 'I'd like a pizza delivered, please.' 'Will that be the usual order, sir?' says the voice on the other end. 'Yes,' says Wenceslas, 'deep pan, crisp and even'.

Or consider these 'classics', drawn from the BBC's Top Ten 'Christmas Cracker' jokes. Did you hear about the two ships that collided at sea? One was carrying red paint and the other was carrying blue paint. All the sailors ended up being marooned. Or, what did the grape say when the elephant stepped on it? Nothing. It just let out a little wine.

For most people, Christmas comes as both a panic and a relief. Some of us go to great lengths to plan it in every conceivable detail, but still many things will happen that will be unplanned. Rather like preparing for the birth of our children, we have a schedule and strategy. But then it just happens. Or it's a bit like football or war. All the tactics are fine and dandy, until the game starts, or battle commences. War and football tend to get complicated when encountering the opposition. Christmas gets complicated when encountering reality, or just family. As I say, it is very much like a birth.

The liturgical countdown to Christmas begins much earlier. The Feast of the Annunciation is on 25 March; this is the moment when Mary says 'yes' to God and immediately conceives. Yet unlike most pregnancies, planned or otherwise, our Lord spends precisely nine months developing during gestation.

It is ironic really that the liturgical year – from the annunciation to Christmas – reflects a level of control hinging on a pregnancy that goes so-according-to-plan. The reality of Jesus' birth is, of course, very different. From the safety of the womb there is no progress to the comfort of a room. Even in infancy, the child messiah is being squeezed out from the world for which he was born. Furthermore, if the Gospels are to be believed, the circumstances of his birth are doubly peculiar – born in an unfamiliar town, and in a stable. It doesn't stop there, either. The homeless family are soon on the run – refugees and asylum seekers (fleeing the wrath of Herod, a jealous local despot), living in Egypt, and with their hospitality.

For many, the reflective space of the days between Boxing Day and New Year comes as a welcome antidote to the overwhelming and frenetic intensity of Christmas. I vividly remember being visited by a pair of speculative Jehovah's Witnesses a few days before I was due to take a crib service, and not long after I'd been ordained. I felt I was rushing from one service to the next at the time: running, just in order to stand still. 'Can we interest you in the imminent return of Christ?', queried the religious cold-callers. 'Help, no', I said, 'not before Christmas – there's no time'. It was a reflex comment, granted. But the slip betrays: despite the apparent space and time to reflect on the deep things – mystery, awe, connections, life – we are often breathless by the consumerism that seems to envelop us all, despite our best intentions.

It is why we have John's haunting reminder in his Gospel that Christmas Day, of all days, is when the light comes to shine in the darkness (John 1.5). When we least expect it, God comes to us. And, moreover, what are we to make of God's extraordinary cunning in sending us such a sublime message about wisdom: that God comes to us as a baby.

Wisdom seems to understand, in the words of the philosopher Thomas Carlyle, that 'under all speech that is good for anything there lies a silence that is better'. For when wisdom comes to us, we are often baffled by its simplicity, not its complexity. At the height of the season and year when we remember light coming out of darkness, we remember – to paraphrase a Chinese proverb – that the darkest place is under the lamp. There can be no gift of light without a shadow. In the past, Christians have always understood this to be the sacrifice of Jesus, and the self-sacrifice and martyrdom of Christians.

So what is Christmas all about? Home is part of its meaning. He has made his home among us. He came to us, and as one of us, and has dwelt with us. He has lived among us, shared our lives, and lived through joy and agony, pain and death, humiliation and celebration. He is Emmanuel: God with us; God among us; God living with us.

In the exquisite novel *The Boy in the Striped Pyjamas* by the Irish writer John Boyne,[15] and in the no less beautiful re-telling of the story in Max Herman's film of the same name, we encounter eight-year-old Bruno and his family leaving Berlin, during World War Two, to take up residence near the concentration camp where his father has just become commandant. Unhappy and lonely, Bruno wanders out behind his house one day and finds Shmuel – a boy in striped pyjamas who lives behind the barbed wire fence, about a kilometre away from the commandant's house.

The boys become friends – an unlikely friendship, indeed – and play games through the wire. Eventually, the German boy Bruno finds a way of getting inside the camp to be with his friend. But in order to really fit in, he asks to put on the striped pyjamas worn by Shmuel and all the other inmates. Shmuel finds him a spare set, and passes them through the fence to Bruno. Bruno quickly dresses like Shmuel, and sneaks into the camp. But before they go back to the hut in the concentration camp, Shmuel asks: 'Are you sure about this ... are you sure you want to do this?' Bruno replies, 'There is no place I'd rather be, and no one I'd rather be with.'

I won't spoil the ending of the book or the film, but you can probably guess how things end for an eight-year-old in striped pyjamas in a concentration camp. But this little scene is all we really need to know about Christmas.

Christmas is God making his home with us. Not just in our churches, but also at home, with us. Christmas is God saying to us: 'There is no place I'd rather be, and no one I'd rather be with.' Because, in his Son, he sends us a simple message of love at Christmas: he is crackers about us. Crackers enough to live, love and die for us. Christmas is simply this: God is at home with us, enjoying us, and loving us more than we can ever comprehend – and for eternity. As we once met face-to-face, so we shall in the end see face-to-face. A famous prayer puts it like this:

'Blessed art thou, O Christmas Christ, that thy cradle was so low that shepherds, poorest and simplest of earthly folk, could yet kneel beside it and look level-eyed into the face of God.'

Abiding 2: an Oxford Christmas

Some years ago, a professor of psychology at the University of Louvain took an interest in how people feasted and celebrated. As part of his research, he asked one of his students to write a thesis on the following subject: 'How do children, aged 9–11 years, experience the phenomenon of *feast*?' The student approached the subject in various ways, and one of these consisted of showing a sample group of 100 children three different drawings of a birthday feast.

In the first drawing, the picture depicted a child alone, but before a mountain of gifts and presents waiting to be opened. In the second drawing, the child was not alone, and was surrounded by just a few members of his or her family alongside some food – a birthday cake, ice-cream, and other treats. But there were fewer presents to open – in fact, only one package, and not a very big one at that. In the third drawing, the child was surrounded by wider family, friends and neighbours, and there was more food. But there was no gift or package in the picture, so nothing at all to open.

The question the children were asked was simple enough: which of these birthday feasts would you rather have for yourself, and why? Seventy per cent of the sample group chose the third drawing, saying that this was the *real feast*. Those opting for the third drawing said, 'Because in the third drawing, everyone is happy – in the first drawing, only I am happy, and in the second drawing, not enough people are happy.'

The children, in other words, grasped something authentic about celebrations: that by only being together can we be truly happy. A true feast, in Christian thinking, is a communion with God, *and* a communion with people – the two are indivisible. And so it is with Christmas. God bids us welcome – to a meal that is collective in character, because God's feasts are profoundly communal. Christmas is the Birthday Feast of Christ.

Most of us have despaired at times over the character of our political deliberations. Sometimes such debates feel like an advocacy for the first two birthday drawings described above: that we are somehow better off on our own, or with just a few people we know well and feel comfortable with. Yet the Christmas Birthday Feast of Jesus is inclusive by nature.

The early Church understood this, so the first Christians looked after widows, orphans and the poor. They treated them not as objects of charity, but as their equals. They did this for foreigners, friends, neighbours, slaves, free, male, female, young and old. As John Chrysostom wrote, '*ubi caritas gaudet, ibi est festivitas*': 'where charity rejoices, there we have the feast'.

So what is there to hope for? 'The Gate of the Year' is the popular name given to a poem by Minnie Louise Haskins. King George VI quoted the poem in his 1939 Christmas broadcast in the early days of World War Two. Most of us know these lines:

And I said to the man who stood at the gate of the year:
'Give me a light that I may tread safely into the unknown.'
And he replied:
'Go out into the darkness and put your hand into the Hand of God. That shall be to you better than light and safer than a known way.'
So I went forth, and finding the Hand of God, trod gladly into the night …

So what of us as we contemplate taking our first steps into a new year? John's Gospel speaks of light in the darkness, and of God 'abiding' with us – a word linked to the word 'abode'.

God, in Christ, comes to dwell with us. He bids us to make our home with him, as he has made his home with us. God is Emmanuel – God is with us. Even when it may all seem dark and hopeless, the light of the world has come.

My brother-in-law Chaz, who lost his life to cancer at 49, lived with us during the final months of his life. Part of my routine during that time was to take him to the doctors, and also do the weekly run to the pharmacy for the morphine and other drugs.

After Chaz had passed away, I went back to the pharmacy with a card and some chocolates, and a very large quantity of un-used drugs that could have sold very well on the black market. The gifts were a simple 'thank you' to Anna and Alison, the two pharmacists who had worked so hard on the dosset boxes of medication, and patiently measured out each day's drugs: fiddly, mundane work that requires concentration and precision. But they had always done it with such cheerfulness, and on the days I had sometimes taken Chaz with me, they were always so good to him too.

So I plonked my shopping bag of drugs on the counter of the pharmacy, conveyed our thanks for all they had done, and handed over the chocolates. We chatted for a while, and I was about to take my leave when they said, 'Wait there please – don't move'. And then they came out from behind the counter and warmly embraced me, in a tender, deep hug of knowing and consoling. So there the three of us embraced in the middle of the local pharmacy. We must have made quite a sight; a most unusual trinity. And in a real sense, that is what Christmas is. God leaves his station, and comes round to our side of the counter. He does not stand apart from us – remaining aloof, as it were, measuring out love and grace behind a distant counter. He enters the world from our side, and embraces us here, in our pain and loss. He knows our losses; he consoles us. He is Emmanuel, God with us.

I had lost my beloved brother-in-law, and here, in this failing, frail, tired flesh of mine, two women held me as Christ might have done. Surely he has borne our griefs and sorrows. Because he has taken on our flesh, and lived among us, and fully as one of us; and loved us in that flesh, and loves us in eternity. This is the meaning of the incarnation. God has come to our side of the counter, and so we encounter him as one of us.

Christmas is God 'one with us': inviting us to be one with another. He has entered our human nature; joined life from our side. Emmanuel. Come: let us give thanks for and share in this Christmas feast. The light of the world has dawned.

Candlemas

Sarah Foot

'Master, now you are dismissing your servant in peace, according to your word; for my eyes have seen your salvation, which you have prepared in the presence of all peoples.' (Luke 2.29–31)

Gospel readings for the Epiphany season focus on different moments when Christ's divinity became manifest. On the Feast of Epiphany itself, we stand with the wise men in the stable and adore the infant Christ. Then we move forward several years from Jesus' infancy to observe his baptism (as an adult), remembering the descent of the Spirit, embodied in a dove, as he rose from the waters, with the voice from heaven declaring God's pleasure in his Son. We mark Christ's first miracle, at the wedding at Cana, and we hear him read from the scroll of the prophet Isaiah in the synagogue in Nazareth, telling the people: 'Today this scripture has been fulfilled in your hearing'. On the final Sunday of Epiphany, the gospel takes us back to Jesus' infancy, to the fortieth day after his birth when Mary goes to the temple for the ritual purification after childbirth required in Mosaic law (Leviticus 12.1–4).

Several themes underlie this familiar reading: we could reflect on questions of purity, or meditate on gender, especially the status of women in Christianity. I find myself struck by the extent to which this passage celebrates old age. Of course, the infant Jesus stands at its heart; his pious parents brought him with them when they went to the temple for Mary's purification and to offer the prescribed sacrifice in thanksgiving for a first-born son. Yet neither the baby nor his parents play the key role in this story. The central figures are the two old people, a man and a woman, Simeon and Anna, both of whom have been waiting patiently for God's intervention and the salvation of Israel. Each recognized Jesus, and each proclaimed him as the Messiah. There must have been other people – other parents with newborns – in the temple at the same time. God could have revealed the truth of Jesus' identity to any of them. But it seems significant that those who saw and testified to Christ's glory were both old, remarkably old indeed, given the average life-expectancy in first-century Palestine.

The books of the Old Testament are filled with people who reached venerable old age, not just the early patriarchs like Noah, Abraham and Isaac, but also many of the prophets who lived what were, for their own times, remarkably long lives. In Ezekiel 43, we read about Ezekiel's vision of Yahweh enthroned in the temple. Ezekiel prophesied for 27 years during the Babylonian captivity and seemingly lived to his fifties, which would have marked him out among his own generation. Prophets needed to live long, for much of their claim to prophetic insight depended on their age, and thus their long exposure to the words and visions of the Almighty. The aged prophets of Israel preserved the past experience of God's people and foretold its future fate.

Yet the fact of the incarnation and the manifestation of the identity of the Messiah to the wise men at Bethlehem, and also to Simeon and Anna in the presentation in the temple, meant that there was no further need for prophets. This infant was the one about whom Moses in the law, and also the prophets, had foretold (John 1.45). John the Baptist would prove to be the last great prophet; with youthful vigour, he would prepare the ways of the Lord and make his paths straight. And with the end of the need for prophets, we find in the New Testament a shift: a shift away from the witness of those who have attained old age, into a narrative carried forward by the actions and energies of the young. John the Baptist, Jesus and his disciples were all men in the prime of life, many of whom would have their lives cut short for affirming their belief in the salvation promised by the Messiah. The particular need the Jewish people had once had for wise prophecy from the elders among them had passed with the coming of the new dispensation.

We encounter in the narrative of the presentation the last two prophets cast in the Old Testament mould. Their age and devotion are the necessary preconditions for their receipt of this marvellous revelation. Both were righteous and devout, regular worshippers and familiar with the law of Moses and the words of the prophets. Anna – who had been living in widowhood to the remarkable age of 84 – spent her time in prayer and fasting in the temple. The moment that she saw the infant, she began to praise God and to speak – to prophesy – about the child to all who were looking for the redemption of Jerusalem.

At this, the final moment when the aged would testify to the meaning of God's actions, we should pause to listen to the testimony of those two old people with some care. A previous revelation from the Holy Spirit had promised Simeon that he would not die until he had seen the Lord's anointed. Taking the child in his arms and gazing upon him, Simeon asserted that he had witnessed God's salvation. His words reinforced earlier passages from Luke's Gospel by affirming unequivocally that Jesus is God's salvation, a light to lighten the gentiles and the glory of God's people Israel. He is the fulfilment of long-cherished hopes, but he also holds a promise for everyone. His message of salvation encompasses all humanity – the gentiles as well as the people of Israel. Then Simeon offered a future-tensed prophecy of his own and the mood of joy and celebration darkened. He turned to Mary to warn her of the grief that was to come, of the rejection and resistance that would dominate Jesus' future, the sword that would pierce his mother's heart.

The deliverance and hope that the infant Christ's birth brings is therefore not a tale of unalloyed joy. The pain and suffering of Calvary are already immanent in this moment of celebration of a first-born's birth. The birth of the Saviour also brings other losses, including the loss of a specific function for the elderly to prophesy the future coming of the Messiah. There are of course old people who play roles in narratives in the New Testament, but they are not nearly so prominent as they were in the Old.

In our culture, we tend to celebrate youth, fame and achievement. Women particularly can struggle to make themselves seen and heard as they get older. Yet, in this story, Simeon and Anna gain their authority to speak to us – and to make us listen – from their long years of devoted service to God. Their example should therefore cause us to reflect on our own attitudes towards those who are ageing, and not just about how to provide for older people financially, or to pay for the social care of those too frail to care for themselves. Broader issues of social justice confront us all, but arguably confront the Church above all, because it has a spiritual responsibility to the ageing. Where does our Church stand on this? How developed is our theology of ageing? When we talk about the demographics of church attendance, we tend to see age as the problem. Mission and evangelization necessarily look at younger age groups, seeking to build congregations for the future. But what about our obligations to the older population, those who have already found a home within the doors of our churches?

A collection of essays edited by Stanley Hauerwas, *Growing Old in Christ*,[16] argues that it is only in the Church that older people can find their rightful role and place. Since Christian communities live by memory, and the central eucharistic feast is a feast of memory, the old have an essential role in the Church. They are the keepers of the meaning, the repository and tellers of the story of the communion of saints. We could profitably reflect on what we do to celebrate and rejoice in their ministry to us, to share in their memories and to listen to their lived experiences of faith and witness to the gospel.

Perhaps our task and opportunity as a Christian community consists precisely in rejoicing for all those in our care, the old as well as the young.

Conversion of St Paul

Martyn Percy

Most of us have realized by now that God appears to have a fairly warped sense of humour. I only have to reflect on the events surrounding my own call to ordained ministry to know that no matter how serious we are, God is never very far from breaking into a wry smile. I first twigged that I might be called to ministry when I was just 16 – a rebellious, recalcitrant and slightly reckless youth. Perhaps not quite the teenager from hell, but definitely one who knew how to put his parents through the proverbial purgatory. Despairing of their eldest, my parents made me sit a two-day multiple-choice career exam to help determine my future. The theory was that if I had a goal in life, I might actually take aim at something. And what did the random tick-this-box formula conclude lay ahead? (1) possibly a career in teaching (this pleased me – a chance to get my own back on the system); and (2) become a clergyman (this horrified me – just how un-cool could this possibly be?).

But the second option stuck – it stalked me like the proverbial hound of heaven. I used to tell people what the results of the careers test were, hoping that they would burst into uncontrollable laughter, and persuade me that I was deluded. But they did not. They would say, 'Oh yes, I can see that', or 'I wondered when you'd realize'. There was no escaping that 'call', and I duly went off to read theology at university and, after a career in publishing, put myself forward for ordination in 1987.

Selection for ordination is an odd thing. My selection conference was at a retreat house in the aptly named village of Offchurch (more humour from God here) – it sounds like an ecclesiastical regulator. Not happy with your vicar? Tired of paying high quotas to your bishop? Want to complain about the preacher? Write to Offchurch ...

My conference went OK. I quickly realized that half the people on the conference were weirder than I was, so guessed the game was up, and that I would soon be swapping my lucrative career in publishing and my beloved MG sports car for the less attractive rewards of a stipend, and the dubious reliability of a Fiat Panda. And so it came to pass. I mention this only to demonstrate that God uses unusual, and perhaps even rather unpromising, material for the priesthood, and to reinforce the point that God clearly has a sense of humour ...

Now, this is hardly a Pauline conversion, or the call of Jeremiah. But the word 'conversion' has its own history outside religion. As a noun, it can mean to change or to switch something. Adaptation, transformation, renovation, alteration or transfer can all be implied in the use of the term. Money can be converted from one currency to another; a small family saloon adapted and converted into a rally or racing car; a barn renovated and converted into a spacious home. But in religious usage, the term tends to denote something else: a radical change, either from one religion to another, or from no religion to the dramatic discovery of faith, and a new relationship with God. When religious people speak of conversion, they normally refer to the idea that – irrespective of their faith tradition – a major and drastic revolution has occurred in someone's life. They are now 'saved'; they have been 'born again'; they are now part of 'the true faith'.

There are good reasons for religious people to understand conversion in this revolutionary way, rather than in the more adaptive and mellow way that the term is normally used in secular language. Consider, for example, Paul the Apostle, one of the first and most dramatic converts to Christianity. The Book of Acts records that Saul (his pre-Christian name) was a zealous persecutor of Christians. But while on the road to Damascus, he has a dramatic encounter – bright light is seen, and the voice of Jesus heard – that makes Saul temporarily blind. He emerges from his blindness as a convert to a new faith. Paul's 'Damascus road experience' (a common phrase drawn from the Bible that has since become part of the ordinary cultural-linguistic furniture) is a typical trope for what many regard as religious conversion: 'I once was blind, but now I see' is how one hymn writer puts it.

But Paul's dramatic conversion is not a typical experience – a template that should frame and judge all other conversions. Paul came to Christianity some years after Jesus is said to have risen and ascended, which begs a question about the other apostles, who had known Jesus in his earthly life. At what point, one might ask, were the disciples converted from Judaism to Christianity? The Bible is somewhat silent on the matter. The resurrection stories suggest that the disciples were fearful and joyful in equal measure, but whatever they made of the resurrection appearances that they were seeing and experiencing, they still attended 'the temple'. At the end of the Gospels, the followers of Jesus are still Jewish, even if, like their master, they are out of sorts with the Pharisees and Sadducees.

Traditionally, the Christian Church dates its birth from the Feast of Pentecost, another dramatic 'conversion' story, in which the disciples receive the Holy Spirit. This may be so, but even in this narrative – also recorded in the Book of Acts – there is no obvious Christian identity to appeal to. Indeed, it is interesting to note that the New Testament at no point gives a definition of what a Christian actually is. Of course, there are hints and clues in stories – 'repent and believe', 'follow Jesus', 'receive the Holy Spirit', 'eat and drink in remembrance of me' – but no formal creed or description by which one can make decisive judgements that include or exclude believers.

That said, the first Christian communities that emerged were marked by difference. When Christians began to understand that their beliefs and practices no longer 'fitted' with the worship of the temple and synagogue, they began to meet in their own homes, just as Jesus and the disciples had once eaten together in an upper room. They chose a modest title to describe these gatherings – the Greek word *ekklesia*, which simply means assembly.

But Christian assemblies were, from the beginning, different. Women would be present – and they might speak too. Children might be there also. Apart from Jews, there might be Greeks, gentiles and other ethnic or national groups. And, most revolutionary of all, slaves were also admitted. In other words, from the very beginning of Christianity its assemblies were radically inclusive. Or, put another way, Christians converted the way that we understand assemblage: their *ekklesia* was for everyone.

Belonging to this community or faith no longer depended on where or to whom you were born; it rested solely on the willingness of the individual, family or other group to be converted, and then to belong. It is also important to remember that for these first 'converts' to Christianity, there was no New Testament, no creeds, and very little in the way of church structures. But it still meant leaving one religion for another. So converting to Christianity, for the first generation of believers, was often a costly business; it meant believing that Jesus was the Son of God, and then being filled with the Holy Spirit – but it could also mean persecution and martyrdom. None the less, it was a simple faith, but with a radical message – and it spread like wildfire.

In her book *Traveling Mercies*, Anne Lamott describes seeing a miracle of conversion at her local church, and it is one that rather surprises her. She relates how a member of the congregation, a man named Ken, was dying of AIDS – his partner having already died of the disease. She writes:

There's a woman in the choir named Ranola, who is large and beautiful and jovial and black and as devout as can be, who has been a little standoffish toward Ken ... She was raised in the South by Baptists who taught her that his way of life – that he – was an abomination ...

But Kenny has come to church almost every week for the last year and won almost everyone over. He finally missed a couple of Sundays when he got too weak, and then a month ago he was back, weighing almost no pounds, his face even more lopsided, as if he'd had a stroke. Still, during the prayers of the people, he talked joyously of his life and his decline, of grace and redemption, of how safe and happy he feels these days ...

So on this one particular Sunday, for the first hymn, the so-called Morning Hymn, we sang 'Jacob's Ladder' which goes, 'Every rung goes higher, higher' while ironically Ken couldn't even stand up. But he sang away sitting down, with the hymnal in his lap. And then when it came time for the second hymn, the Fellowship Hymn, we were to sing 'His Eye Is on the Sparrow'. The pianist was playing and the whole congregation had risen – only Ken remained seated, holding the hymnal in his lap – and we began to sing, 'Why should I feel discouraged? Why do the shadows fall?' And Ranola watched Ken rather skeptically for a moment, and then her face began to melt and contort like his, and she went to his side and bent down to lift him up – lifted up this white rag doll, this scarecrow. She held him next to her, draped over and against her like a child while they sang. And it pierced me.[17]

Conversions don't just happen to people on the outside of the Church. They happen on the inside too – to you and me. But what do we need converting from and to? What dazzling light and voice from heaven does it take to get us to change? And where will God take us next?

Having a laugh (in Lent)

Carol Harrison

It might well be thought that laughter isn't very fitting in Lent. In fact, we don't often laugh in church (unless we're suppressing a fit of giggles when someone says or does something untoward). There isn't much laughter in Scripture either and, as far as I'm aware, neither Christ nor his disciples are recorded as laughing.

But there are some notable exceptions. In Genesis 17, God promises Abram that he will make an everlasting covenant, with him and his descendants, throughout all generations. He promises that Abram will be 'exceedingly fruitful', the father of nations, and that thereafter he will be called Abraham. Abraham's reaction to God's promises is to fall on his face; to prostrate himself before God – no doubt he was literally bowled over by the prospect, overcome by awe that God should make such promises to him of all people, and perhaps also moved by fear and incomprehension.

But when God then proceeds to promise that Sarah (previously called Sarai), Abraham's wife, will be the *mother* of nations, that they will together be the forebears of kings and that Sarah will bear him a son, his awe, fear and incomprehension turn to laughter. We are told that Abraham's reaction to the promise of a son was again to fall on his face, but this time he 'fell on his face and laughed, and said to himself, "Can a child be born to a man who is a hundred years old? Can Sarah, who is ninety years old, bear a child?"' (Genesis 17.17). Clearly, the very idea is just too much for him and he collapses in helpless laughter – a laughter that expresses incredulity at the absurdity of it all; disbelief at something so beyond the stretch of the wildest imagination. But God is insistent: Sarah will bear a son, and they are to call him Isaac – significantly, a name which in Hebrew means 'one who laughs'. So, we first of all learn of Abraham's laughter of disbelief and incredulity, but there is more laughter to come.

Next, it is Sarah's turn. Three visitors arrive (we'll come back to them later) and God repeats to Abraham the promise of a son, this time in Sarah's hearing. Sarah's reaction is again to laugh. She is old – ancient – and way beyond the years of childbearing, and so she laughs to herself, saying 'After I have grown old, and my husband is old, shall I have pleasure?' (Genesis 18.12). Like Abraham's laughter, there is a large dose of disbelief and incredulity in Sarah's private laughter, but there is also, I think, a hint of joy and delight, when she imagines being able to conceive a child. This must have been beyond her wildest dreams: she was barren and when she had despaired of ever being able to have her own children, she had agreed that her husband should father a child with her slave. That Abraham should once again sleep with her, and that she would bear their child, seemed impossible but also irresistibly delightful – and so she laughed.

Whereas God overlooked Abraham's laughter, he comments on Sarah's. What follows is a rather extraordinary conversation. God, sounding almost hurt, says to Abraham, 'Why did Sarah laugh, and say, "Shall I indeed bear a child, now that I am old?" Is anything too wonderful for the LORD?' (Genesis 18.13–14). God has not commented on the element of secret delight in Sarah's laughter, but only drawn attention to its lack of confidence in his power. When Sarah, now afraid, denies that she laughed, God is even more hurt and says 'Oh yes, you did laugh.'

Sarah's secret delight, which God missed in her first, rather ambiguous laugh, becomes an unmissable, exuberant, resonating cry of joy when Isaac, her promised son, is born. She is consumed by delight and exclaims – no doubt choking with laughter – 'God has brought laughter for me; everyone who hears will laugh with me … Who would ever have said to Abraham that Sarah would nurse children. Yet I have borne him a son in his old age!' (Genesis 21.6–7). This is a very different laughter: a laughter not only filled with joy and delight but also with confidence, recognition, affirmation and acknowledgement. God has fulfilled his promise; he has revealed his power; he is to be trusted and believed. Sarah's infectious laughter is his witness, and anyone who hears it cannot remain unaffected by it; they will laugh 'over her' and 'with her', and share her joy. Of course, there is still a deep undertone of incredulity and disbelief, but this time it is expressed not as doubt, but as wonder.

It is here that I would like to return to the mysterious three figures who, in between Abraham falling on his face in laughter, and Sarah's ambiguous laughter, visit them by the oaks of Mamre. The three are clearly a very thinly veiled way of depicting the Lord's presence, and God's voice becomes theirs. In later Christian tradition, this episode was interpreted as a revelation of God the Holy Trinity, the Father, Son and Holy Spirit, as in the famous Trinity icon by the Russian painter Andrei Rublev, where three angels are seated together, united in mutual recognition.

The identity of Abraham's three visitors remains mysterious and hidden; they are not mentioned by name – and the point is that this is precisely how God's nature is understood, then and now. For the divine nature will always be incomprehensible; it will always transcend human understanding: it is the un-nameable 'I Am Who I Am' of Exodus. But this ineffable God is also a God who makes himself known to us; who reveals himself in human terms, and in human history, through very human figures. He is, as we have just seen, the 'God of Abraham, the God of Isaac and the God of Jacob'. His actions may well challenge or subvert human expectations and certainties, but this is how we are brought to wonder – and laughter (sometimes in incredulity and disbelief; sometimes in joy and delight) at his transcendent, limitless power and greatness.

In fact, there is a sense in which everything we say of God is a bit of a joke. He cannot be defined and described, and when we try to say something about him we are always forced to resort to all-too-human images, analogies and metaphors; to saying: 'this is what God is like', not 'this is what God is'. So, for example, when theologians have tried to describe the threefold, trinitarian nature of the One God, they have resorted to talking about human nature and three human beings; to one light made up of three overlapping suns; to someone who speaks, his word and his breath; to water that runs from a source, through a stream, into a river; to a tree that begins with a root, grows into branches, and produces shoots. These analogies are at once absurd, but are the best we can do. We can never say precisely *what* God is, only *that* he is, on the basis of his revelation to us.

This telling of jokes, of course, isn't one sided: as we have seen, God also tells jokes, he makes people laugh, and in the process jolts them into faith in what seems absurd; hope for what seems unrealizable; love and delight for his extraordinary works. God is, in fact, a consummate comedian: what seems far-fetched, impossible, or just plain foolishness is more often than not his way of making us laugh: there was a 90-year-old and a 100-year-old who had a son; there was a virgin who conceived by the Holy Ghost; there was a stable in Bethlehem where God was born in the hay; there was a wedding in Cana where water was changed into wine; there were two women whose brother was brought back to life after three days.

These all sound like the beginnings of a joke: one that catches the attention by recounting something absurd: a joke that first of all invites a confused laughter of incredulity, then – as it progresses – a hesitant, uncertain laughter, in which incredulity is mixed with hope; and then, when what seems absurd actually happens, invites the full-throated, exuberant laughter of recognition; of wonder, joy and delight. What is impossible for men is possible for God; what is foolishness for men is wisdom for God.

The bridge between incredulity and joyful wonder is not, however, crossed by understanding anything, but by faith, hope and love, which delights in God and his ways, even though they will always defy human comprehension.

So, I would like to suggest that we should all become Isaacs, children of Abraham and Sarah, one who laughs. We need a sense of humour to believe in the unfathomable, foolishness of God, and to take joy and delight in his jokes. For if we take things too seriously, and try to explain the joke, we will miss it altogether!

Palm Sunday: what does it take not to bend?

Nigel Biggar

When we enter cathedrals and churches on Palm Sunday, and are handed innocent-looking palm crosses, in accepting them we are identifying ourselves with the 'crowds' that rapturously welcomed Jesus into Jerusalem. We side with the Good Guys, the ones who cheered Jesus on, and – according to Matthew 21 – the ones who scared off the chief priests and Pharisees from arresting him.

The problem is that, as the Passion story has it, the 'crowds' changed their tune. The Good Guys turned bad. And by the end of the story, by the end of Holy Week, they – and we who bear their palm crosses – will be baying for Jesus' blood. The point is sharply captured by Samuel Crossman's famous Passiontide hymn, 'My song is love unknown', whose third verse runs thus:

Sometimes we strew his way,
And his sweet praises sing;
Resounding all the day
Hosannas to our King.
Then 'Crucify!'
Is all our breath,
And for his death
We thirst and cry.

Now, that's an emotionally powerful thought, especially when it's sung. But perhaps it's also a bit melodramatic. After all, what have *we* to do with jeering crowds?

The Passion story, in which we are all involved during Holy Week, presses us to think again. It presses us to consider that we have more in common with baying crowds than we might suppose. Furthermore, it presses us to consider that what we have in common is *weakness*.

As I read it, the Passion story suggests that weakness is the root of evil as much as – maybe more than – sheer malice. Certainly, malice played its part in Jesus' murder, for later in Matthew's Gospel we are told that when the chief priests were interrogating Jesus, 'they spat in his face' (Matthew 26.67).

But if the malice of some is the motor, the weakness of many others is the vehicle; and the Passion story is full of instances of weakness – first of all, the disciples at Gethsemane who couldn't stay awake and then, in panic, fled; Peter's failure of nerve and his threefold denial; the 'crowd' who stopped waving palms and started waving their fists; and finally Pilate's shrug of the shoulders.

Yes, there was malice, but there was also weakness in spades.

There are, of course, many different kinds of weakness, and many different causes of it. So let's stick with the weakness that inclines us to follow the crowd, to go with the flow, or at least not to stand against it.

One cause of our weakness is obvious and familiar – usually, we just want to avoid trouble. When a storm is blowing most of us, most of the time, simply want to keep our heads down, to get by, to survive. After all, we've got families to care for, we've got jobs to hold on to, we've got important projects to develop, we've got services to run, we've got sermons to write, and we just don't want the world outside to disrupt our private lives and the genuinely valuable things to which we devote them. And besides, what difference could *we* possibly make?

My sympathy for those who keep their heads down was deepened some years ago, when 12 miles north of Berlin I was standing in the middle of what remains of Sachsenhausen concentration camp, where prisoners of war and Jews were murdered during the Nazi period. As I looked towards the neat suburban bungalows that lined the street leading up to the camp's front gate, I thought to myself, 'Suppose I had lived over there, then, and suppose the reality of what was happening in here had begun to press itself upon me, what, exactly, would I have done? What, exactly, *could* I have done?'

We stand here in a morally grey area, somewhere between prudence and cowardice. On the one hand, discretion *is* often the better part of valour. On the other hand, there is somewhere a bottom line, on the far side of which valour becomes the better part of discretion. So while we may sympathize with those who averted their eyes, kept their heads low, and either followed the crowd or let it flow around them, we cannot but admire – and be challenged by – those who didn't.

And in Nazi Germany, some did not. One of the most moving sights in Berlin is the Memorial Museum of the German Resistance,[18] which comprises a dozen or so rooms, each devoted to a different group of resistance – here the churches, there the trades unions; here youth organizations, there student groups – and in each room the walls are covered with photographs, snapshots of men and women, adults and adolescents, most of them perfectly ordinary.

One of the dissidents who has impressed me most was not so

ordinary. He was an aristocrat called Helmuth James von Moltke, who seven decades ago found himself organizing one of the most famous anti-Nazi resistance groups in Germany, the so-called Kreisau Circle. During the war, von Moltke worked as a legal adviser in military intelligence in Berlin, from where he wrote regularly to his wife, Freya, several hundred miles away in Silesia.

In a letter written in October 1941, von Moltke gave anguished expression to his own sense of moral weakness:

> Since Saturday the Berlin Jews are being rounded up. They are picked up at 9.15 in the evening and locked into a synagogue overnight. Then they are sent off, with what they can carry. A woman known to a friend of mine saw a Jew collapse on the street: when she wanted to help him up, a policeman stepped in, stopped, and kicked the body on the ground so that it rolled into the gutter: then he turned to the lady with a vestige of shame and said:
>
> 'Those are our orders.'

> How can anyone know these things and still walk around free? With what right? Is it not inevitable that his turn will come too one day, and that he too will be rolled into the gutter? – All this is only summer-lightning, for the storm is still ahead.

> If only I could get rid of the terrible feeling that I have let myself be corrupted, that I do not react keenly enough to such things, that they torment me without producing a spontaneous reaction. I have mistrained myself, for in such things, too, I react with my head. I think about a possible reaction instead of acting.[19]

Don't we all?

But von Moltke did have a bottom line, and he did resist. On 7 March 1940, he described to Freya an unusually fraught day at the office:

> There was a big row and I wonder whether they'll decide to throw me out at last. Once more I was defeated on a decisive question [about the treatment of prisoners of war]. When the

meeting was over I asked permission to exercise the right of every official to have his dissenting opinion put on record. Big row: I was an officer, I was told, and had no such right but simply the duty to obey. I said I was sorry, but this was a question of responsibility before history, which to me had priority over the duty to obey. The matter came before the admiral, and after five minutes he endorsed my opinion. He obviously had shared it all along, at any rate had wavered, and my resistance had strengthened his courage. Result: the admiral will have his personal dissent recorded in the minutes and will also speak to these minutes before Hitler.[20]

What does it take to resist? What does it take to swim *against* the stream? What does it take to stand up, and to stand out? The Nazi judge who condemned von Moltke to death on 10 January 1945 knew what it took. 'From whom do you take your orders?', he asked during the trial. 'From the Beyond or from Adolf Hitler? Who commands your loyalty?'[21]

What it takes to step out from the crowd, what it takes not to sway now this way, now that, is heeding the claim of an Authority beyond, beyond the esteem of our social peers, beyond the requirements of a quiet life.

Isaiah 50.4 makes the same point: 'The Lord GOD has given me the tongue of *a teacher* ... Morning by morning he wakens – wakens my ear to listen *as those who are taught*' (my italics). The ability to teach – and here we're talking about *prophetic* teaching, teaching by speaking out and speaking against – is a function of being taught. Taught by whom? By the Lord God, by the Beyond, by an Authority that transcends our ordinary, natural, secular loyalties, and calls us to risk everything, that we might gain everything. It is because he acknowledges the Lord God that Isaiah is able to stand out and apart: 'The Lord GOD helps me ...', he writes, 'therefore I have set my face like flint' (50.7, my italics).

Which brings us, by allusion, back to Jesus, of whom Luke's Gospel tells us that 'he *set* his face to go to Jerusalem' (Luke 9.51, my italics). As with Isaiah, Jesus' power to stand out from the crowd was fuelled by his openness to God, an openness he trained himself in by regularly withdrawing to pray. Many is the occasion in his Gospel when Luke tells us that Jesus withdrew 'to deserted places' (5.16) or 'went out to the mountain' (6.12) to pray 'alone' (9.18); and, indeed, he was in just such a place on the night that he was arrested.

So if we are to become the kind of people who are capable of standing up and out, of resisting rather than conveying evil, then it seems one thing that we should do is to follow Jesus in withdrawing regularly to a place apart and beyond – beyond the insistent and all-absorbing desires and demands and hopes that trammel ordinary life – in order to create space to hear the voice of God. That, of course, is what Lent is especially about, with its deliberate abstention, its deliberate interruption of the ordinary rhythms of desire and satisfaction.

But having withdrawn to listen, what are we told on Palm Sunday itself? We're urged to think again about what we have in common with the fickle crowd – one moment waving palms, the next moment waving fists. We're urged to consider whether we bend too much with the wind; to note the evil that such bend-ing can assist; to observe, in Jesus, that resistance is possible; to confess our weakness and pray to God for the strength to stand in the time of trial, and to tell the truth, come what may, be it in Jerusalem, in Berlin, or in any other city, town or village.

Happily for us, this downbeat word of judgement is not the *whole* word of God; but it is part of it, and it is salutary. For the rest, we must delay gratification, and wait until Easter Sunday.

Holy Week

Carol Harrison

> Guard me as the apple of the eye; hide me in the shadow of your wings (Psalm 17.8).

Easter is the beginning of the period of 50 days leading up to Pentecost, in which we celebrate the glorious resurrection of Christ from the dead and rejoice in the hope of eternal life. The beginning of spring in the northern hemisphere, with the lengthening days, greening trees, flowering bulbs and buds, coincides beautifully with the time when we emerge into the light, life and beauty of Eastertide.

And yet during the week between Palm Sunday and Easter Day, I have sometimes found myself recollecting the shadows of Holy Week: the candelabras flickering in the dark womb of a cathedral during Compline; the incense curling up into the vaulted half-light; the candlelight around the altar of repose in the lady chapel, gently cradling and enfolding our Lord's body on Maundy Thursday, all in the cold darkness of a cathedral stripped bare.

Sam Wanamaker Playhouse in London is a reconstruction of an indoor Jacobean theatre (a theatre that would therefore have been built at the same time as many pulpits) just next to the Globe, on the South Bank. In defiance of all health and safety regulations it is built almost entirely of wood and lit solely by candles – candles carried in candlesticks, set into wall sconces, or held in huge candelabras that rise and fall. The pools of light, the shadows and edges of darkness, the shifting reflections of things half-seen and half-heard, add so much to the drama that it is difficult to imagine the play in the electric light of a modern theatre.

In the Sam Wanamaker Playhouse we are drawn into what is being enacted and made part of it by the shadows; by the way the light is more immediate, more human, and yet also more seductive and mysterious, implicit and complicit, because it is created by a glowing, flickering candle that temporarily dispels the surrounding darkness. When something that is difficult to enact takes place – a murder or, as so often in bloody Jacobean tragedy, the blinding of someone or the cutting off of a limb – the candles in the Playhouse are snuffed out and the audience is simply left in complete darkness to imagine what is taking place, and of course the effect is to make the unseen action even more real and horrendous.

The edges of darkness; half-light and shadows; glowing pools of light are the context in which the dramatic events of Holy Week are played out in churches. But often I am reluctant to leave the shadows of Holy Week because of the devotion of Tenebrae – literally, the service of shadows. It was originally part of the monastic offices of Lauds and Matins for Maundy Thursday,

Good Friday and Holy Saturday. The first set of readings are taken from the Lamentations of Jeremiah, where the fall of Jerusalem to Nebuchadnezzar is bewailed, the plight of Israel bemoaned, and all is sighing, suffering, despair and desolation. The refrain is repeated: 'Jerusalem, Jerusalem, return unto the Lord your God'. Sometimes there are three settings of the lamentations by the eighteenth-century French composer François Couperin: his *Trois Lecons de Tenebres*. These are gloriously, stunningly, unspeakably beautiful. Apparently, when the opera in Paris was closed during Lent, the audience would decamp to church to listen to Tenebrae instead! But I mention this devotion not so much to confess my sins, or my gratitude to the musicians, or even my admiration of our Precentor's French, but to reflect on the shadows.

Such a devotion will usually be lit by six candelabras and, as each lamentation comes to an end, the canons' verger will appear, bearing a large brass candle-snuffer to extinguish each candelabra in turn. Lamentation by lamentation, churches are cast into deeper and darker shadows until, at the end, all that remains is a single light: the flame of the Paschal candle from the Easter before, flickering in front of the altar. Following tradition, this is then taken behind the altar, so that the darkness becomes complete; the desolation, despair and anguish of the lamentations seeming to have overwhelmed the faltering light. Then, after the glorious music and the glowing lights, the congregation is cast into silence and darkness. But in the darkness there often begins a banging, a knocking, a rattling, a drumming ... the ground shakes, the air reverberates, the silence is shattered, and the darkness lifts as the candle is brought back before the altar.

What is happening? The congregation is, somewhat unusually, stamping its feet, and making as much noise as possible, emulating the ancient practice observed by monks in the eleventh century. People are shattering the silence and dispelling the darkness of sin and death, and regaining the light of hope and life.

On Maundy Thursday, churches and cathedrals celebrate the liturgy of the Last Supper, once again in the shadows. In Durham Cathedral they re-enact the ceremony of the Judas cup: the chapter, divested of their vestments save for their black cassocks, gather around a table. The dean, representing Christ, says, 'Truly I tell you, one of you will betray me – one who is eating with me'. Each of the assembled asks 'Lord, is it I?' Then a cup is passed from one to the other in silence. Having drunk, they affirm: 'Even if I have to die with you, I will never disown you'. The ceremony then ends with the words 'It was night', whereupon the lights and candles of the cathedral are extinguished and the building becomes as the night – a night in which Christ *will* be betrayed, and in which all we are able to do is to keep watch into Good Friday.

Some years Easter is so early that Good Friday coincides with the Feast of the Annunciation. The death of Christ on the cross and his burial in the tomb coincides with the day on which we recall the conception of Christ by the Holy Spirit in the womb of Mary. It is impossible not to draw parallels: the conception of Christ in the flesh and his death in the flesh; the darkness of the womb which would bring him forth in birth, and the darkness of the grave from which he would rise on the third day; the movement from darkness to light.

But the darkness of the womb, like the darkness of the tomb, is not a darkness of absence, sin, or death but a divine darkness, a darkness of the mystery of God, 'immensity cloistered in thy dear womb', a presence in absence. It is like the darkness in churches and cathedrals on Holy Monday when the candle is taken behind the altar; the darkness on Maundy Thursday as we wait for Good Friday; the darkness when Nicodemus came to see Christ at night; the darkness when Moses reached the top of Mount Sinai: it is the deep but dazzling darkness of divine presence; the darkness in which we can best conceive what we can never fully see or know: the glory of God.

Above all, it is a pregnant, fecund darkness, ready to spring forth, to be born, to rise again, to erupt into the world with new life. It is the miracle of the virgin birth; the miracle of resurrection from the dead; the miracle of Noah's ark being saved from the flood; the miracle of Jonah, three days in the belly of the whale and then brought forth alive; the miracle of dying to sin and rising to new life in baptism. In all of these miracles the passage to new life is not a straightforward, easy one; it does not really follow the course of nature: rather it disrupts it; overturns it. It requires suffering, the shedding of blood, earthquakes, darkness over the face of the earth, floods, drowning, burial, the veil of the temple to be torn in two: only so, only through these seismic shifts and shakings, it seems, can we move from darkness to life. The harrowing of hell on Holy Saturday captures this drama of darkness. This is the moment when some churches observe the same practice observed at Tenebrae: the congregation makes a fearful banging, clanging and clattering with whatever is to hand, marking the shifting of the ground, the rolling away of the stones, the breaking open of the tombs, when Christ descends to free the dead from their graves. Once again, the darkness is full of drama, pregnant with meaning, a necessary means to light and life.

And so in Holy Week when we celebrate the light and new life of the resurrected Lord, we should remember that it is only in and through darkness that this light and life can be grasped; that the darkness is necessary; the shadows are not to be feared – for it is only in and through them that we can bear to enter the blinding brightness of God's glorious presence and hide under the shadow of his wings.

Reading the ascension

Martyn Percy

To test liberalism a little, I want to offer two interpretations of the ascension. The first 'reading' is more akin to the liberal bishop John Shelby Spong's brand of liberalism, who is sometimes described as 'being on the cutting edge of nineteenth-century theology'. The second reading is more a new liberalism, like my own.

Spong's reading would go something like this. According to two of the Gospels (Matthew and Luke), Jesus and his disciples arrive at a mountain some 40 days after the resurrection. After a few brief words, Jesus departs on a cloud, and disappears into heaven. Ten days later, 50 days after the resurrection, Pentecost follows, and the bereft disciples, deprived of their guru, are transformed from a small sectarian community into a fledgling church. Ascension is one of the most problematic doctrines for Christians to cleave to. For it seems to require the suspension of intellect, and to ignore almost everything we know about the world and the universe. It was obviously no problem for the disciples of Jesus to believe, as other Jews did, that beyond the sky lay the kingdom of heaven, as much as below the earth lay the realm of the devil.

Another more obvious reason is that awareness of the universe invites us to read the Gospel accounts in a different way. Clearly, the enemy is literalism. Bishop Mervyn Stockwood used to regularly tease his evangelical clergy around Advent. 'I know you evangelicals', he would say. 'Out in your back gardens this time of year, gazing at the stars through your telescopes, looking for Jesus.' But however Matthew and Luke are to be read, their stories about the ascension (or imminent return) of Jesus cannot be regarded as 'history' in any conventional sense, nor as mere description. To read the stories in this way would be to miss the richness of the authors' intentions.

For example, Spong says the story of Jesus' ascension compares favourably with that of Elijah from the Old Testament, except that the Gospels make bigger claims for Jesus. This is not surprising, since the Gospel writers regard Jesus as the Son of God, whereas Elijah is simply a prophet. Thus, Elijah gets to heaven via a chariot of fire; Jesus, on the other hand, needs no such assistance (the function of the cloud is actually to hide him from view). Elijah left a 'double portion' of his anointing to his understudy, Elisha. In contrast, Jesus leaves the Holy Spirit for the Church.

Spong asserts that the Gospels contain a number of these Old Testament re-workings, suggesting that the stories we have been left with need to be regarded in a more subtle light. However, this does not mean that the stories are in any sense 'untrue' – on the contrary. The Gospels explain the unexplainable – miracles, resurrection, ascensions – in first-century terms, in ways that made sense to Palestinian, Hellenistic and Jewish audiences. The cosmology we are given is not false, but rather true in its time. Anyway, it is only the background to the central truths that lie in the foreground of the picture. Just as the Psalms of the Old Testament suggest that the earth is flat and the sea full of Leviathans, so do the Gospels of the New Testament divide their world between Hades, earth, sea, sky and the heavens. We may laugh at this now, but some measured humility is due. The cosmologies we now accept as 'true' are relatively new, and they remain incomplete and contestable.

My reading of the ascension, however, takes a different line, which is recognizably liberal, but also orthodox. The starting point can be the same as Spong's, but the working out is different. I might begin with a question too: can a human being fly? How are we to imagine Jesus as he gently steps off the mountain and, instead of falling, rises? It doesn't seem to be a problem for Jewish or Christian theology. Elijah is carried to heaven; so is Enoch. Jesus ascends. And as recently as 1950, Pope Pius XII wanted us to believe that Mary, the mother of Jesus, had not died, but had been assumed into heaven.

At first sight, the idea of ascension looks risible to modern minds. As Carl Sagan once remarked to Jack Spong, if Jesus literally ascended, then we should still be able to see him travelling through space, even if he is moving at the speed of light. And how did he cope without oxygen at 20,000 feet? Did his resurrection body gasp for air, or didn't he need it? Furthermore, where is this 'heaven' that Jesus is journeying towards? Past Mars, turn left, and keep going until you see the Pearly Star Gates? It is quite clear that the biblical account of the ascension will not endure the fierce heat of post-Copernican cosmology. The picture in the Museum of Atheism in Moscow is right: a spaceman drifts alone in the solar system, beholding the earth. 'You see', says the caption, 'there is nothing up here – not even God'.

But to try and read the ascension in this way is wrong. Indeed, I am critical of Spong here – on the ascension and resurrection – for not being faithful to the subtlety of biblical narrative. Some is history, but there is analogy, poetry and doctrine as well. Spong's strategy is to read the Bible like a fundamentalist, and then declare that it doesn't work. Well, if we start from there, I agree with him: this is part of his cavalier appeal. But of course we shouldn't really begin there at all. Stories of the ascension and resurrection are not meant to be read 'scientifically', historically or literally in the ways that others might be. Genesis 1—3 is not in competition with Charles Darwin, Stephen Hawking or Richard Dawkins: the narratives serve different purposes. Jesus' ascension does not violate air traffic control; as we shall see, its purpose is to tell another story – about God and us.

Liberal thinkers are quite right to suggest that the language the Bible uses is not 'literally' true: it is figurative, imaginative and poetic. But orthodox thinkers are also right: this language is the only thing we have to speak about God. One of the tasks of theology is to try and take the figurative and scriptural and re-convey it in a more literal fashion. But of course it is not to, strictly speaking, translate one language into another, so theologians can tell us what to believe. It is more subtle than that. Theologians are not translators – they are grammarians. As such, their charge is to point out the nuances and subtleties in the language, in order to let the Christian imagination grow into what is already 'revealed', so that the Church can then begin to articulate, though only *begin* mind, what are essentially and remain mysteries.

And so to the ascension. What do we make of it? Luther thought that the ascension made Christ *more* present to the world; freed from bodily constraints, he could now 'fill all things', as Ephesians 4.10 claims – the Word made flesh was now the Cosmic Christ. However, attractive though Luther's thinking is, Calvinists criticized him for lapsing into the Eutychian heresy. This heresy, condemned at the Council of Chalcedon, claimed that Christ's human body was 'swallowed up' on his entry into heaven. But why is this heresy?

It is important to understand that the ascension is primarily a doctrine for the Church, not a historical fact. The story of the ascension is an attempt to tell of what Christians felt to be significant about Jesus: as with most of the New Testament, this consists of equating, conflating and celebrating the divine and human nature of Jesus. The early Church took the view that although Christ was physically absent, his resurrected body – and himself – none the less continue in heaven. It is this raised body that will judge the living and the dead. The doctrine of the ascension is, then, a story of absence, not newly configured presence. The enfleshment of God – our human nature in the divine – remains this side of the parousia. In other words, it is the ascension that creates the fulcrum for salvation history. Christ's absence means that God's mission is entrusted to the Church, in the power of the

Spirit, in union with Christ – until he comes again. The departure – for that is what the ascension is – is the cue for mission to begin; it does not begin at the resurrection.

To see the ascension as doctrine and not history, of course, simply takes away the problems of 'history' and relocates them in cosmology. Where did the disciples think Jesus' body was? Where was heaven in a first-century mind? The answer is not nearly as simple as writers like Spong suppose. One Hellenistic line saw the universe as being made up of carefully ordered concentric spheres: the earth at the centre, thence through the elements, past the stars and planets, until you reached the empyrean – the boundary. Beyond the boundary no mortal could pass; this was not heaven, as Plato argued, but beyond heaven.

For Plato and Aristotle, whatever was beyond the boundary was timeless and placeless, and therefore the arena of God. However, this 'other place' was always more, in classical minds, than simply the layer above the sky; the view is more subtle than that. Aristotle and Plato described their ideas of 'heaven' in different ways, but it is clear that neither thought of a crude triple-decker earth-sky-heaven scenario. Their heaven was incorporeal, and could not, strictly speaking, be said to be 'up there' – a point reiterated by Philo and Origen. Aristotle and Plato differed on what could inhabit the heavens, and how the heavens related to the spheres they understood as having matter. However, what is clear is that when a phrase like 'above the highest heaven' is used, something illusory and metaphysical is being described, not something spatial and temporal.

How does this connect with Jesus going up, up and away? Well, the writer to the Ephesians (4.10) does not mean Jesus is just beyond the stars, floating around in space with the planets. What the ascension means is this: a material body has gone to an immaterial place that does not exist in space, and cannot be journeyed to. For the early Christians this meant that, daringly, the incarnation, in a real sense, continues. Christ is the man in heaven: the ascension is therefore the reverse of the incarnation – for just as Christ *descended* into the world, Jesus has now ascended *outside* the universe. Of course, this doctrine is a paradox, and the bravery of it would have shocked the classical mind-set. The idea that the corporeal could exist in the incorporeal would have been as strange as the idea that 'God became flesh'. In other words, the ascension is an *acosmic* event: a doctrine to be believed in, not a historical 'fact'.

So the ascension is, in a way, a negative doctrine. It takes Christ out of the world (but not out of resurrected flesh), and demands faith, not knowledge. This is why it is wrong for us to read the ascension as a crude account of a departing God, or as bad literalism; in actuality, the story is a very sophisticated vehicle for a very important doctrine.

The whole point of the ascension is that it is the end-game of the resurrection. We do not know how God is this or that: the ascension says, literally, that Christ has 'passed beyond human knowledge'. Whatever cosmology is in place, Christ remains outside it: so to follow Jesus is to pursue a mystery.

The Swiss theologian Karl Barth tells us that Jesus is 'the way of God into the far country'. The ascension is the doctrine that begins our journey of faith, because we are forced to admit that the combination of cosmology and history cannot describe how Jesus is for us. The doctrine proclaims that the truth is not our possession; that Jesus is not an object immediately present to our rationality or senses. Gnosis is taken away – to make way for faith.

This is why Christ's absence calls for faith, not knowledge. Truth is now deferred until he comes again. In the meantime, Christ is present in sacramental and ecclesial life. But even here, as Paul reminds us, 'now we see in a mirror, dimly, but then we will see face to face. Now I know only in part; then I will know fully' (1 Corinthians 13.12).

Pentecost

Sarah Foot

Whitsun, White Sunday, is the late Old English name for Pentecost, the seventh Sunday after Easter, the fiftieth day after Easter Day, which is what the Greco-Latin name 'Pentecost' means. It is one of the major feasts of the Christian year, and it celebrates the occasion of the Holy Spirit descending upon the disciples; it also represents both an end and a beginning. Pentecost marks the end of the Easter season, the period when the risen Christ remained among his disciples. It is a moment of leaving behind what is past (most vividly reflected in Christ's physical departure from the world and his ascension into heaven).

But Pentecost also launches something new: it marks the formal initiation of the Church's mission to the world: 'If you love me, you will keep my commandments. And I will ask the Father, and he will give you another Advocate, to be with you for ever ..., the Spirit of truth' (John 14.15–17). This gift of the Spirit is the fulfilment of that promise Jesus made to his disciples: 'I will not leave you orphaned' (John 14.18).

In his narrative in the Book of Acts, Luke located the gift of the Spirit as coming on the day of the Jewish festival, the Feast of Weeks, when the firstfruits of the wheat harvest were presented and Moses' giving of the law commemorated a festival that fell 50 days after Passover: 'When the day of Pentecost had come, they were all together in one place. And suddenly from heaven there came a sound like the rush of a violent wind ... Divided tongues, as of fire, appeared among them, and a tongue rested on each of them. All of them were filled with the Holy Spirit and began to speak in other languages, as the Spirit gave them ability' (Acts 2.1–4).

We might recall here John the Baptist's prophecy as recorded in Luke (3.16) that Jesus would baptize with 'the Holy Spirit and with fire'. Because of its direct association with new life, in the early Church the Feast of Pentecost was the other time of the year – that is, in addition to Easter Eve – at which catechumens (new converts to the faith) might be baptized. The English name

'Whitsun' probably derives from the white clothes that the newly baptized used to wear for the eight days after their baptism. In the Middle Ages, Pentecost was considered a suitably solemn date for royal coronations, with the royal anointing of the king in that ceremony acting as an outward sign of the reception of the Holy Spirit. The newly crowned king would thus be rendered both Christ-like and a vessel of God. Pentecost, or Whitsun weekend, is also a popular occasion for weddings, as described by Philip Larkin in *The Whitsun Weddings*.[22] This poem is about the transition that marriage makes – entirely appropriately as this season is characterized by change, when the gift of the Holy Spirit effects its transformation on each of us.

The gift of tongues given to the disciples, which Luke here interpreted as the ability to speak in different languages, but that Paul tended to explain as the uttering of incomprehensible babble, baffled the crowd who witnessed it. Some of the sceptical present wondered if the disciples were drunk, just as – were this event to occur in a contemporary context – we might wonder if the apostles' ecstasy were chemically rather than spiritually induced.

But Peter's speech, as recorded in Acts, explains that it is not that the disciples are out of their minds, but that the prophecy of Joel is being fulfilled. And then he repeats much of the text from the Book of Joel, 'I will pour out my Spirit upon all flesh, and your sons and your daughters shall prophesy, and your young men shall see visions, and your old men shall dream dreams' (Acts 2.17).

Quite when the Old Testament prophet Joel was writing is unclear, but what is obvious from his own text is that he wrote in response to a devastating invasion of locusts that swarmed over all the crops of the fields but also over all the people in their houses. He interpreted this plague as a sign of judgement of the Lord and urged the need for the Israelites to repent, and throw themselves on the mercy of God.

That petition seems to have been successful, for God has sent the autumn rains and, as the newly planted crop sprouts, the hope is offered of full granaries once more, repaying what have clearly been years of famine. But then the prophet moves into eschatological mode; he starts talking explicitly of the last things: 'Then afterwards I will pour out my spirit on all flesh' (Joel 2.28). The young will prophesy and see visions, old men will dream dreams, and God will show portents on heaven and earth, turning the sun to darkness and the moon to blood, all prefiguring the coming of the 'terrible day of the Lord'. There will be those who escape – specifically those who call on the name of the Lord – but the portents for Joel are, none the less, predominantly forecasts of destruction and death.

Yet on Peter's lips in Acts 2.17, this prophecy becomes a declaration of new life. Note how Joel's 'then afterwards' became on Peter's lips 'in the last days' (2.17). For Peter, the wonders that Joel prophesied were fulfilled in the life and deeds of Jesus' ministry on earth; what is being prefigured now is the second coming with its latent promise of the redemption of humankind.

This vividly evocative passage in Acts 2 reminds us of the limitless possibilities available to most young people in the Western world. For many – though by no means all – everything is possible as they stand on the threshold of adult life: they have 'vision'. They are leaving behind that which is past and launching forward into something that may now be starting to be revealed. But for the old, such visions are past: 'your young men shall see visions, and your old men shall dream dreams'. The old have their memories, they can dream about their own youthful visions and reflect on their past glories, but their futures are narrower, less fluid, more closed as the reality of the imminence of mortality can less and less be ignored.

But Pentecostal fire touches each of us – young and old. And touched, we too are changed. Wherever we stand, on the threshold of adult independence, in middle years, or at the end of life, every year Whitsun takes us back to this pregnant moment in the life of the people of God and the relationship between God and his people: us. For the gift of the Spirit fulfils Christ's promise to all of us, his children; it confirms what he told us in his life and in the time he was among his disciples after his resurrection, that his purpose is our redemption, our salvation. The coming of the Spirit shatters expectations, while Christ's ascension seemed to bring an end; we now have another beginning, a promise of new life: 'everyone who calls on the name of the Lord shall be saved' (Romans 10.13).

Pentecost – Whitsun – is about the changes that arise from the outpouring of God's grace and power. The Spirit touches all our lives, young and old alike, effecting a transformation from which we cannot emerge unchanged. In ending, I return to my beginning. In Larkin's *The Whitsun Weddings* that we mentioned earlier, the railway journey acts as a metaphor for the journey of life, a journey each of us makes, and to which, whatever our life stage, we can all relate.

Transfiguration: a meditation

Martyn Percy

There are two occasions in the Christian year when we hear the gospel message describing the transfiguration. The first is on 6 August, the Feast of the Transfiguration. The second is on the Sunday before Lent. Both work well. The gospel looks forward to the very end of Lent – Easter Sunday – when the son of man is glorified and raised, dazzling. But the feast day also shares another anniversary: that of the *Enola Gay* over Hiroshima, Japan, on 6 August 1945. A cloud, a dazzling light. The transfiguring in a weapon of mass destruction.

When we read the story of the transfiguration, the first thing that might strike us is its strangeness. There is a dazzling light – but yet a cloud. There is revelation – yet things are hidden. There is a voice – yet we do not know what is truly heard. Clouds are common imagery for divine presence, and they serve an ambiguous purpose: to remind us that the revealed remains hidden; that the extraordinary comes to us in the ordinary.

In a mirror image to the gospel, Elijah puzzles over the presence and absence of God. Surely God will be in the earthquake, or the wind, or the fire? But no; God is in the silence. God does not shout; God whispers. And here we sense what I think of as the *thick sound of silence* in God's heart, as he waits for Elijah to be fully attentive.

In today's world we are bombarded with noise, and silence is rare. But there are many kinds of silences. In the gospel, Jesus and three disciples break away from the crowds and the hubbub to get some peace, quiet and calm. It is in this context that the transfiguration happens; in a place of solitude and quiet. The transfiguration story ends when Peter speaks, and it is the end of silence that breaks the spell.

Just as there are many kinds of silence, so there are many types of listening. A Church cannot be a teaching Church unless it is a learning Church. A Church that speaks cannot truly speak unless it can listen, but the listening that God asks of us is a deep listening. In the words of that famous song, we need to learn to listen to 'the sound of silence'. Deep prayer is founded on the discipline of deep listening.

I often wonder how the transfiguration story might have looked if Jesus had taken three different people with him up the mountain. Say, for example, Mary Magdalene, Luke, and perhaps another? I wonder, first, if the vision would have been interrupted by any of them, as Peter did in the transfiguration. And I wonder if anyone else would have suggested a building project, as Peter suggested: 'let us build three booths'. Typical. To every epiphany, mystical experience or revelation, there is someone on hand to turn it into a religion. But this course is rejected by Jesus. Building three booths is pointless. God is not going to be cooped up in a booth with his friends. Peter's response, as on other occasions, shows a remarkable lack of understanding. He should listen and watch; but he talks, and tries to build.

In the middle of this ex-stasis – standing outside oneself – Peter's instinct is to routinize, memorialize and religionize. Let us enshrine the experience. Let us have raiments that are white and glisten; incense for clouds, the apostolic succession of Moses, Elijah and Jesus. Let us make a memorial and a place for the ethereal. Let me speak; let me build. But Peter is only required to do one thing: watch, and say nothing; to listen. It is interesting that the moment Peter speaks, 'a cloud overshadowed them' (Matthew 17.5). And that Peter only spoke because he didn't know what to say.

The story of the transfiguration is of course about learning to live with the cloud *and* the light, and learning that the voice of God comes in quiet ways. Our demand for a sign is, more often than not, childish. This is partly what this encounter in the Gospels is all about. There is the bread that we eat, and there is bread … the bread that truly feeds us. God wants us to cultivate a patience and a stillness that can truly discern the depth of his presence, and can truly listen. It is no accident that the transfiguration story ends with these words: 'this is my beloved Son; *listen* to him'. So often, it is what we *don't* do.

But what is deep listening? Several things come to mind. First, it is about the development of a slow, patient spirituality. In our Pot-Noodle-Just-Add-Water world, we expect instant results, instant nourishment and instant answers. But spirituality is a slow business; it's a gentle marathon, not a sprint. Listening comes about by becoming attuned to the silent, subtle voice of God. It is often mellifluous. It is about real bread.

Second, deep listening comes through deep relationships. It is about a depth of attending to the other. It is not a technique, but part of a committed relationship in which there is a willingness to give of ourselves, and also receive. It is born of desire – deep desire – to both know and to be known.

Third, it is about restraint. For someone to speak, someone must be silent. And for someone to speak, there must be someone to listen. Being listened to fully is a deep privilege, and although we often presume that God will listen to us in prayer, it is rare perhaps for us to expect God to speak to us, and for us to listen. We need to be silent.

In the stillness, we sometimes have the opportunity to pause and reflect more deeply than perhaps we normally do on the space we need to be still. It can be a time when we resolve to say less and listen more – to each other, and to God. This is important, because sometimes what seems natural and obvious to us is not what God would have us do. The transfiguration story cuts through our plans, words and activities, and says powerfully: 'listen'. Above all, we are sometimes asked to wait. We cannot hear God in a microsecond; we have to stop so we can engage and hear. It takes time and space – without distraction.

But what of Elijah in all this? Well, wildernesses are often places of encounter and wrestling, but also of escape and refuge. We think of Jesus in the wilderness, making ready for his ministry: the ultimate retreat, with no distractions, but plenty of discerning and testing. For Elijah, this confounding continues all the way to his hiding place on Mount Tabor. It is here that Elijah hopes God will speak to him dramatically and clearly. But as 1 Kings 19.11–12 says:

> Then the LORD said: 'Go out and stand on the mountain before the LORD, for the LORD is about to pass by. Now there was a great wind, so strong that it was splitting mountains and breaking rocks in pieces before the LORD, but the LORD was not in the wind; and after the wind an earthquake, but the LORD was not in the earthquake; and after the earthquake a fire, but the LORD was not in the fire; and after the fire a sound of sheer silence.

When he heard this, Elijah hid his face in his cloak and went out and stood at the entrance of the cave. A voice said to him, 'What are you doing here, Elijah?'

The Hebrew phrase translated as 'a light, silent sound' is not quite right. A better phrase might be the 'thick silence' I mentioned previously. And sometimes this is indeed how God speaks to us in the wilderness. More often than not, we don't get clear directions in response to our desperate petitions, let alone for our most childish prayers and pleas. We get the 'thick silence'; the response that says, in the wilderness, look around you, and see what God has already provided. God often wants us to see that his provision is to be found in the places that we distrust, or even despise. Or that our future – as we imagined it – is what God will give us if we keep asking for that. God has other plans, sometimes; other futures for us to embrace. This is the lesson for Elijah in the wilderness, and often for us too, when all seems barren and beyond redemption.

What God asks for, then, is that we are open in heart and mind in the wilderness, and not clammed up and bitter – as Jonah became for a while, and as Elijah might have become. Being open is the key, but to imagine that being open-minded is the way forward is to miss the point. Being open to God's grace and abundance is not simply a matter of being more liberal in our thinking. Rather, being open leads us to a richer place of generosity. If we can learn to receive from the people we would rather disdain, God will teach us not only of his generosity, but also something of how we might become open and generous through his grace.

Waiting for God can often mean being available to God in silence. In Christian ministry, we can often become absorbed with doing – this is, ultimately, Elijah's problem, and Peter's. They are both activists, and used to seeing the hand of God in works and wonders. But as for hearing God, they have yet to learn of his deep silence – the conduit through which he speaks. So the lesson for all of us is to stop doing, and take time to listen. The presence of God is in the cloud; the voice and the light are behind it. It is in the sound of silence that we can begin to hear the stirrings of God. It is in waiting that we are directed.

Michaelmas: Feast of St Michael and All Angels

Martyn Percy

And he dreamed that there was a ladder set up on the earth, the top of it reaching to heaven; and the angels of God were ascending and descending on it. (Genesis 28.12)

The next day Jesus decided to go to Galilee. He found Philip and said to him, 'Follow me.' Now Philip was from Bethsaida, the city of Andrew and Peter. Philip found Nathanael and said to him, 'We have found him about whom Moses in the law and also the prophets wrote, Jesus son of Joseph from Nazareth.' Nathanael said to him, 'Can anything good come out of Nazareth?' Philip said to him, 'Come and see.' When Jesus saw Nathanael coming towards him, he said of him, 'Here is truly an Israelite in whom there is no deceit!' Nathanael asked him, 'Where did you come to know me?' Jesus answered, 'I saw you under the fig tree before Philip called you.' Nathanael replied, 'Rabbi, you are the Son of God! You are the King of Israel!'

Jesus answered, 'Do you believe because I told you that I saw you under the fig tree? You will see greater things than these.' And he said to him, 'Very truly, I tell you, you will see heaven opened and the angels of God ascending and descending upon the Son of Man.' (John 1.43–51)

Michaelmas – the feast that celebrates the angels of heaven and their ministry – is one of the strangest Christian festivals. For who can ever say they have seen an angel? Actually, many tend to do just that these days – but that is a discussion for another time. In the Scriptures, angels usually bring disruptive news – hardly tidings of great joy. Their presence and their announcements prompt trauma and soul-searching. They take the small and meek and make them great and strong. They tend not to take 'no' for an answer. Angels are not to be messed with. They are God's ambassadors: here to convey God's stipulations and conditions for surrender and action. They are not here to negotiate terms. So I think it is fair to say that if we want to understand the story of Jacob's ladder in Genesis, we need to know why Jacob is on the run, and where he might end up. As with so many stories in the Old Testament, the meaning is locked up in words and phrases that are often lost to us. Jacob is feeling the wrath of his older brother, Esau. He has already deprived Esau of his birth-right, and now by deception – pretending to be a hairy man rather than a smooth man – he has taken the blessing that their father, Isaac, would usually have bestowed on the older son. Esau is furious at the trickery. But Jacob, although he now has become the son and heir, flees for his life.

Genesis is careful to give reasons why this might not be such a bad thing. Esau has intermarried with the Canaanites. God, it seems, and Isaac too, do not approve. The fidelity of Jacob – even with his trickery – seems to be preferred. But Jacob is now on the run, and he heads from Beershava (or Beersheba – meaning the well of the oath) to Haran, which simply means 'parched'. So from a well of water to a place of thirst is the journey Jacob now takes. Haran is in modern-day Turkey, and this journey is no picnic. It is in Haran that Jacob himself is tricked by Laban into marrying Leah, when he wanted Rachel. The wages of sin are simply expressed in the Old Testament: what goes around comes around.

It is in this context – between Beersheba and Haran – that Jacob has his dream. He's on the run, and he's clearly no angel himself. Indeed, Jacob's name means, in Hebrew, 'one who walks crooked'. As he is named, so he lives. And yet this extraordinary dream or vision is one of daring provision in the midst of fear and flight, and of God's generosity and grace. The angels are the silent messengers in this story, before God speaks, with these final, extraordinary words: 'Know that I am with you and will keep you wherever you go' (Genesis 28.15). Jacob may be in flight, leaving everything and everyone, but God does not abandon us.

One of the reasons why the stories of the Old Testament are so likeable is that the characters are all quite flawed: the good, the bad and the ugly are all mixed up. And frequently the resolution and salvation for individuals is to let go and let God. We can think of Jonah on his sulky journey to Nineveh, or any of the other prophets who come and go. But God is Lord of the Journey.

In a rather strange film by Bruce Joel Rubin, called *Jacob's Ladder* (1990), we meet a man called Jacob Singer who loses all his friends in combat in the Vietnam War, and wakes up several years later to find that he is a postman in New York. He doesn't remember how, and the rest of the film is devoted to recovering memories and flashbacks. At a key moment, Jacob's friend Louis cites the fourteenth-century Christian mystic Meister Eckhart:

Eckhart saw Hell too. He said: 'The only thing that burns in Hell is the part of you that won't let go of life, your memories, your attachments. They burn them all away. But they're not punishing you', he said. 'They're freeing your soul. So, if you're frightened of dying and … you're holding on, you'll see devils tearing your life away. But if you've made your peace, then the devils are really angels, freeing you from the earth.'[23]

To some extent, this is the experience of the biblical Jacob too. It's only when he lets go that he really begins to experience the blessing of God. Like many clergy, I have spent a good deal of time sitting with people who are preparing to die. It is, unfailingly, a moving experience: both profound and a privilege. I particularly recall spending time, as a curate in Bedford, sitting with a frail old lady in one of the many nursing and residential homes in the parish, as she moved gently from this life into the next, only occasionally recovering consciousness to talk about her hopes and fears, and about her faith.

One day, she told me a story of how she had met an angel. The year was 1970 – and Enoch Powell had made his famous 'rivers of blood' speech just 18 months earlier. Bedford was fertile territory for Powell's cultural concerns – a place that had welcomed many immigrants from Asia, Africa, the Caribbean and the Far East in the postwar era – yet was also a rather conservative county town. Tensions were very apparent, and trouble was brewing.

The frail old lady, who was by now slipping into the next life as I held and stroked her hand, told me of how she had gone down to the town hall one evening in winter, to attend a meeting for residents who were concerned about the growing number of immigrants. It had been an uneasy few hours, with impassioned speeches and much angst.

Then it ended, and she stepped outside, only to discover the town covered in a thick blanket of fog – a real pea-souper, courtesy of the River Ouse. But she made her way to her little Morris Minor and, as she was unlocking the car door, a large man appeared from behind, and gripped her tightly to himself. She did not know how, but she had caught just enough of a glimpse of him to know that he was black, weighed about 15 stone, and was about six foot two.

But he held her from behind so tightly that she could hardly breathe. She could not scream either. Yet she found herself feeling unusually composed, and then, for what seemed like an age but can only have been a few seconds, she realized the man was weeping. She struggled for breath, but found herself asking him what was wrong.

He replied, through sobs, that he was hopelessly lost. He had just arrived from Caricou – a small island in the south of the Caribbean – and had never seen fog or mist like this. He was afraid. His grip relaxed and, slightly to her amazement, she found herself driving him across town, where she dropped him off. When they got to the address, he turned to her and said that he had prayed to God that night – that he would send an angel to guide him to his family, living on the other side of town, miles from the railway station. And that God had answered his prayer. After he had left, the woman broke down in tears, and went home.

As she told me the story, I asked her why she had remembered this, and especially now. Because, she said, he had prayed for an angel to guide him. But in actual fact she was no angel. Rather, he was the angel God had sent to her: he was the stranger in disguise. The man made her confront her fears; she realized that the strangers she was being taught to fear needed help and welcome – that *she* could entertain an angel. We can perhaps see what Meister Eckhart means now. The things that grip us tightly are for loosening. The demons tend to clench and grip, but angels help us to let go; that is why Mary can say 'yes' at the annunciation.

Which brings us, neatly enough, to St Michael. He is an interesting character; he is not like other saints – because he is an angel. There is no date or place of birth. He is a 'shared saint' too – common to Christian, Jewish and Muslim traditions, who all revere him in slightly different ways. But here's the thing. Michael's name means, literally, 'one who is like God'. So the leader of the angels is the one who is most like God.

A popular story from World War Two tells of a Romanian Christian who found himself imprisoned at Belsen, and deprived of all he needed to sustain his faith: no crucifix, Bible, icons, devotional books, corporate worship or knotted prayer beads. So he prayed in secret – that he might respond to the call of love. He found himself spending time in the camp with the sick, the starving, the diseased, the dying and the betrayers – all those who were shunned by others.

One day, as the camp drew close to liberation, an atheist – a priest, in fact, who had his faith shattered by the experience of war – came to see the Romanian and said, 'I see how you live here. Tell me about the God you worship.' And the Romanian replied: 'He is like me'. I wonder which of us could ever reply: 'he is like me'? The call to discipleship remains compellingly simple: to be like him. And yet we often miss saints when they are right under our noses, because they can be very ordinary people – just like us.

According to one Jewish tradition, we are all in the hands of God, but it is the righteous souls who 'glow like sparks in the stubble'. It is an enchanting image. Saints, rather like the embers of a fire, continue to give off light and heat, and may still illuminate life. But they are also thrown out of the fire into the world. They are on loan here, setting light to life, but illuminating us with their wisdom and holiness. Although they are dead, it is because of their deeds that they are not forgotten. But their lives – sacred, selfless and sacrificial – still speak to us today, and ask us what we think life is really worth living for.

To answer this, we have to look into our hearts, and ask some searching questions. What random and costly acts of kindness and generosity will we perform today? Can we love and serve others – putting them before ourselves – and yet not count the cost? Can we, at the same time, radiate warmth, peace, openness and hospitality? Can we be beams of God's light and warmth in a world that is sometimes dark and cold? Can our friends and colleagues say, hand on heart, that to know us is to somehow have been touched by the presence of God?

And that is what commemorating St Michael and All Angels is all about. The encounter between Jesus and Nathaniel in the New Testament is all about recognition: 'you are the Son of God'. It is about seeing beyond the apparently obvious, yet right through to the simplicity of what God places before us. But the Feast of Michaelmas is also about the angels – and our potential. Can we be God's messengers? Can we, like Michael, be one who is like God? It's also about all our vocations. Can we let go of the things we cling to, and cling to us, and become freer to be ourselves, love God and serve others? Can we ever, like Michael, and like the priest in the prison camp, say of God, 'he is like me'? It may seem like hard work, but we need to remember what God says to Jacob: 'Know that I am with you and will keep you wherever you go' (Genesis 28.15).

St Luke

Carol Harrison

Whole cities reverberate, resonate, echo and re-echo and swarm with the ringing of great cathedral bells. There is no ignoring it: it fills the air and the ears; strikes buildings and the body – everything seems to vibrate with sound, is possessed by it. I love cathedral bells: the disorder in order; the waves of clashing sound that, through the ears, flood the mind and body and overwhelm them. They are one of the glories of ancient churches.

When I went to an Orthodox Ethiopian liturgy in Jerusalem the effect was the same: this time the voices of the congregation rang out in the most extraordinary polyphony. Each person seemed to begin singing at a different time, their voices rose and fell in what sounded like a random rhythm of endlessly reverberating praise – again, a sea of sound in which the listener could not but be caught up, consumed and made a part of. Ambrose, the fourth-century bishop of Milan, describes the singing of the Church with a wonderfully poetic image that captures this effect beautifully: 'the Church ... hums with the prayer of the entire people like the washing of waves, and resounds with the singing of psalm responses like the crashing of breakers'.

When we celebrate St Luke, the only author in the Bible to write a two-book narrative (unless you also include the Holy Spirit's inspiration of the Old and New Testaments), we are celebrating Luke's Gospel and the exciting sequel that follows hard on its heels – the Acts of the Apostles. Luke's story not only looks *back* to the birth, life, teaching, passion, death and resurrection of Jesus, the Messiah, the fulfilment of the Old Testament, but also to his own *present*: to the time after the descent of the Spirit at Pentecost, to the sending out of the apostles to preach, to convert and to baptize all nations; to their heroic evangelism and their lives as travelling missionaries, teaching, preaching, persuading and arguing for the gospel of their resurrected Lord, whatever the cost. But, of course, Luke must leave his story unfinished – there is no resolution in Acts: no conversion of the world or second coming; no last judgements and no final persuasion of hostile

Jews, Romans and gentiles. Rather, Acts ends with Paul awaiting martyrdom, acknowledging that Isaiah was right: the word of
salvation had fallen on deaf ears, blind eyes and hard hearts. Now
it must be preached to the whole world.

So two volumes: looking back to the past, recounting and
reflecting on the present in the light of that past, and anticipating
a future that Luke must leave to others to write. Rather like the
sound of church bells, in Luke's writing the past re-echoes, resonates and reverberates consuming the lives of those who hear it in
the present moment, uniting them, filling their hearts and minds,
and converting their attention inexorably towards it. But it also
presses on into the future: it cannot be ignored, it is not resolved,
there is no final coda; it continually re-echoes, moving onwards.

Luke understood his own role as someone who keeps that
sound alive: someone who hears, receives and hands on what has
been handed on to him by 'those who from the beginning were
eyewitnesses and servants of the word' (Luke 1.2). It's odd that
he speaks of 'eyewitnesses ... of the word'. Like the other evangelists, he provides no visual detail about Jesus' life and teaching;
rather, he is preoccupied with continuing to make it heard, to
echo and re-echo in his own present. Luke's Gospel and Acts are
packed with sayings, stories, sermons, speeches – words; insist-
ently repeating, over and over again, in many variations, like a
peal of bells, the good news inspired by the Holy Spirit; endlessly,
joyfully sounded forth by apostles, so that all who hear it might
also be caught up in it, consumed by it, and have their lives transformed by it.

Isaiah also invites his hearers to participate in this sort of sound:
it is a sound, he tells us, that comes from God; a sound that fills,
feeds and satisfies the souls of those who incline their ears to God
and listen carefully to him; a sound that is not just water, but wine
and milk for the thirsty; not just bread, but rich food for the poor,
but only if they attend to God, listen to him and delight in him; a
sound that, once uttered, does not return empty but fulfils God's
purposes.

It is, in short, a sound very much like Luke's Gospel. Describing
the mission of David, Isaiah uses words that Luke almost directly
re-echoes in describing the sending out of the apostles in Acts:

'you shall call nations that you do not know, and nations that do not know you shall run to you' (Isaiah 55.5).

Above all else, this is a joyful sound – an exuberant sound, a sound of good news. As Isaiah puts it: 'For you shall go out in joy, and be led back in peace; the mountains and the hills before you shall burst into song, and all the trees of the field shall clap their hands' (Isaiah 55.12).

It is not a sound that consists primarily of ideas or arguments, a sound that requires a considered, well-thought-through response. The transcendent God cannot ultimately be expressed in these terms. As Isaiah puts it: 'my thoughts are not your thoughts, nor are your ways my ways' (Isaiah 55.8). But we can hear God, in the sound, as one poet puts it, of 'the whizzing of a pleasant wind'; in the proclamation of Christ's salvation and deliverance, in the rushing of the Holy Spirit, endlessly reverberating in the words of the evangelists and apostles, converting and possessing its hearers, provoking cries of joy, the clapping of hands, and confident witness.

T. S. Eliot, describing the way in which we can be possessed by what we listen to, wrote that 'you are the music while the music lasts'. So we must listen to the gospel almost as if we were listening to church bells. We must incline our ears to hear those who sound forth the good news: to Isaiah and the prophets; to the evangelists; to Luke and the apostles; to priests and preachers; to the voices of worship, praise and song. We must be caught up in their rhythm and repetition, overwhelmed by their sound, consumed by delight, love and longing for the God they proclaim. But, above all, we must allow this sound to resonate, to enter not only our ears but our minds, bodies and souls; to feed us and inspire within us faith, hope and love so that we stretch out, with delight and longing, towards its inspiration and end: God, the Father, Son and Holy Spirit.

Bible Sunday

Martyn Percy

> Teabing smiled. 'Everything you need to know about the Bible can be summed up by the great canon doctor Martyn Percy.' Teabing cleared his throat and declared, 'the Bible did not arrive by fax from heaven ... the Bible is a product of *man*, my dear. Not of God. The Bible did not fall magically from the clouds. Man created it as a historical record of tumultuous times, and it has evolved through countless translations and revisions. History has never had a definitive version of the book ... More than eighty gospels were considered for the New Testament, and yet only [four] were chosen for inclusion ... The Bible, as we know it today, was collated by the pagan Roman emperor Constantine the Great ...'[24]

Well, like much else in Dan Brown's novel *The Da Vinci Code*, the passage above is nonsense. But writing as the person quoted in the above extract, I guess I ought to try and clarify my views a little. It is true that 'the Bible is not a fax from heaven' is a quote correctly attributed to me, although to the best of my knowledge I have only ever said this in lectures, radio, TV and newspaper interviews – all in connection with understanding fundamentalism. But behind the slick sound-bite, there is in fact a fairly sophisticated theological point. Let me explain.

Views about the authority and status of Scripture cannot be directly resourced from the Bible itself. The Bible has no self-conscious identity. As a collation of books and writings, it did indeed come together over a long period of time. Indeed, the word 'Bible' comes from the Greek *biblos*, meaning 'books'. Equally, the word 'canon' (here used in relation to Scripture, not as an ecclesiastical title) simply means rule. So the Bible is, literally, 'authorized books'. But the authorization of the compilation took place after the books were written. It should be clear that Paul, when he wrote 'all scripture is inspired by God' (2 Timothy 3.16) in a letter to his friend, Timothy, could hardly have had his own letter in mind at the time. The conferral of canonical status on his letter came later – some would say much later.

My point is simple. Views about the authority and status of the Bible cannot be solely resourced from the Bible. The Bible needs to be held and understood in a particular way, independent of its content, in order to have any authority. Furthermore, behind such a view is some kind of nascent notion of how the power of God works in the world. For some (perhaps especially fundamentalists), the power of God must be mediated through clear, pure and easily identifiable channels or agents. This guarantees the quality of that power: it is unquestionable and unambiguous.

But for others – usually of a more mainstream, broad or perhaps liberal persuasion – God acts and speaks through channels and agents that are fully themselves. So God works through culture, peoples and history, not over and against them. The almighty power of God is only ever known on earth partially (not absolutely); it can only be encountered 'through a glass, darkly' (1 Corinthians 13.12, KJV) and not 'face to face'.

So although the power of God may be pure and absolute at source, God *always* chooses to mediate that power through less-than-perfect agents (such as language, people, times and places). And this is because God's primary interest is in disclosing his love in order to draw us into relationships, and not in unequivocal demonstrations of power, which would leave no room for a genuinely free response, but merely obedience in the face of oppression. So we have the burning bush for Moses – but he covers his face. And although Jesus is the light of the world, 'the darkness comprehended it not' (John 1.5–9, KJV), according to John. What is revealed is still 'hidden' to those who are blind.

But how does my 'fax' quote relate to the Bible? Simple. Some Christians believe that Scripture has come from heaven to earth, in an unimpaired, totally unambiguous form. Such views are fundamentalistic: the Bible is the pure word of God – every letter and syllable is 'God breathed'. So there is no room for questions; knowledge replaces faith. It is utterly authoritative: to question the Bible is tantamount to questioning God.

But to those who believe that Scripture is a more complex body of writings, the authority of Scripture lies in the total witness of its inspiration. Thus the Bible does indeed contain many things that God may want to say to humanity (and they are to be heeded and followed). But it also contains opinions about God (even one or two moans and complaints – see the Psalms!); it contains allegory, parables, humour, histories and debates. The nature of the Bible invites us to contemplate the very many ways in which God speaks to us. The Bible is not one message spoken by one voice. It is, rather, *symphonic* in character – a restless and inspiring chorus of testaments, whose authority rests upon its very plurality. The Scriptures are like sausages – delicious, nourishing and tasty – but you really don't want to see how they are made.

So, when Paul tells us in 2 Timothy 3.16 that '… all scripture is inspired by God …', he is not talking about himself. For the early Christians, the 'scripture' Paul refers to may have meant the Old Testament, and perhaps what they knew of the Gospels. But it didn't mean the New Testament because, as a settled volume or concept, it did not exist until the fourth century – the same time that the creeds crystallized. But is it true to say that the New Testament is 'the work of man'? In one sense, yes: people had to write the texts – they were not faxed! But on the other hand, there is a case for arguing that the Church only chose authentic and faithful records that testified to Jesus accurately, and history bears this out. As Archbishop Michael Ramsay once remarked: 'the Bible is a consequence of Christianity, not its cause'.

But what does any of this have to do with the words 'all scripture is inspired by God'? The answer, I guess, is in what we make of this curious word that we use all the time about quite a lot of things. The word is, of course, 'inspiration', which in its original Greek usage literally meant 'god-breathed' – *theo-pneutos*. Obviously, there are many kinds of inspiration, but the question arises: what kinds of inspiration does God use? A burning bush may seem 'obvious' to you – but to others? Remember the lines from Elizabeth Barrett Browning's poem:

> Earth's crammed with heaven,
> And every common bush afire with God,
> But only he who sees takes off his shoes;
> The rest sit round it, and pluck blackberries.[25]

Inspiration, then, is not about re-stating the obvious. It is about receiving the breath of God; hearing his whisper; seeing his shadow. I am always wary of groups or individuals who claim 'to be biblical', because in my experience this kind of exclusive, tribal claim is exactly the kind of thing the Bible doesn't offer us. In fundamentalist worlds, it is never the Bible that rules; it is always the interpreter. So that's why we read Scriptures together – because this is a shared journey of adventure and discovery in which the simple can confound the wise, and the foolish outwit the clever. So Scripture – like art, music, poetry, symbols and signs – invites us to sit a while and contemplate. The burning bush of Moses has no single meaning. It is an invitation to pause and look more closely; step through the gates of mystery that God provides for each of us. It is in contemplation that we find depth and wisdom; and, with that, love and breadth. God did not send us a 'fax' (as in the extract from *The Da Vinci Code* on p. 96), or even an email, but rather his Son, born of a woman. The light shines and the fire burns; and some people are struck by its beams of radiance. But the rest, as Elizabeth Barret Browning says, carry on picking blackberries. That is why we need to be generous to one another when we read the Bible together, for we all see God differently. As the writer Brian McLaren has put it:

Generous orthodoxy is ... the practice of dynamic tension – [resisting] the reductionist temptation to always choose one thing over another, [learning] to hold two or more things together when necessary ... Anglicans have demonstrated this beautifully in relation to scripture ... it is never *sola* [scripture]. Rather, scripture is in dialogue with the tradition, reason and experience.[26]

And this is why we are ending with George Herbert, and his famous poem on the Holy Scriptures – note the plural – taken from *The Temple*, 1633:

Oh Book! infinite sweetness! let my heart
Suck ev'ry letter, and a honey gain,
Precious for any grief in any part;
To cleare the breast, to mollifie all pain.

Thou art all health, health thriving till it make
A full eternitie: thou art a masse
Of strange delights, where we may wish & take.
Ladies, look here; this is the thankfull glasse,

That mends the lookers eyes: this is the well
That washes what it shows. Who can indeare
Thy praise too much? thou art heav'ns Lidger here,
Working against the states of death and hell.

Thou art joyes handsell: heav'n lies flat in thee,
Subject to ev'ry mounters bended knee.

Oh that I knew how all thy lights combine,
And the configurations of their glorie!
Seeing not onely how each verse doth shine,
But all the constellations of the storie.

This verse marks that, and both do make a motion
Unto a third, that ten leaves off doth lie:
Then as dispersed herbs do watch a potion,
These three make up some Christians destinie:

Such are thy secrets, which my life makes good,
And comments on thee: for in ev'ry thing
Thy words do finde me out, & parallels bring,
And in another make me understood.

Starres are poore books, & oftentimes do misse:
This book of starres lights to eternall blisse.

So the Bible lights the way – it is bright and illuminating for us.
Brighter even than the stars. The Bible cares for us, loves us and
judges us. The word of God does exactly what God would do
with us. It speaks to us, and draws us deeper into communion
with him – our maker, redeemer and friend.

Christ the King

Carol Harrison

The Feast of Christ the King celebrates not only Jesus of Nazareth, the son of a carpenter but also that of Christ the King. The question of how we relate the two persons is rather like the early Christian debates on the union of Christ's humanity and divinity: it is not an easy one to answer.

To begin to reflect on it I would like to follow the example of prophets, evangelists, teachers and preachers across the ages – indeed, of God himself – and turn things upside down; subvert them and work with opposites.

Take the statement: 'humility exalts; pride casts down'. It captures a fundamental truth in powerful, provocative antitheses. Humility exalts. Why? Because we must always remember that, of ourselves, we are nothing; that we owe everything that we are to a Creator who brought us into being from nothingness and literally gave us the breath of life; that we are completely and utterly dependent upon him, not only for the fact that we exist at all, but that we continue in existence and do not fall back into nothingness.

The truth is that we cannot forget this fact: we temporal, mutable creatures must always humbly acknowledge the source of our being; we must always be aware of our need and our utter dependence on the one who, in his loving and generous abundance, has given us life; we must always humbly look to the source of all goodness with faith, thankfulness, trust, hope and love. Only in this way are we exalted or lifted up.

On the other hand, pride casts down. If we forget our Creator and think that we are self-sufficient; that we can take things into our hands and do very well by ourselves; if we are tempted to turn away from God, to ignore him and to trust to our own resources, then we fall. We lose the source of our lives and move back towards the nothingness from which we came; we are diminished and incline towards death. In our pride we are cast down.

So, humility exalts; pride casts down. How does this subversive truth relate to Christ the King, who we celebrate today?

The title 'King' is very much like many of the other titles that Scripture uses to refer to Christ's earthly, incarnate ministry – titles such as shepherd, door, lamb, light, bread. In other words, it is really a very human title, an earthly analogy, used by us to try to express something of our belief that the man Jesus, the son of a carpenter, and himself a carpenter, is also the eternal, immutable Son of God. What better way can we find to express this than to give him the highest human role we can imagine: a king, a ruler, someone to whom people owe obedience, allegiance and service.

In other words, calling Christ 'King' is our attempt to express our belief that Christ isn't like us at all: he isn't created from nothing by God; he *is* God. We affirm this when we say the creed and express our belief in 'One Lord Jesus Christ, the only begotten Son of God, begotten of the Father before all worlds; light from light; very God from very God; begotten not made, of one substance with the Father, by whom all things were made.'

Yet these statements of faith are precisely that: a confession of what we believe rather than of what we can understand. For, of course, God himself can never be comprehended by human minds or articulated in human words. Instead we use analogies, which we must always remember are simply the best we can do in human terms – Father, Son, light or King.

These are all terms that, when we apply them to God, inevitably turn things upside down; subvert things; work with opposites. 'King' conjures up a ruler, someone with authority, an earthly kingdom of power and subjection, someone to whom we owe obedience and allegiance, someone to whom, if called, we would give our life. This is what Pilate feared when he heard Christ's enemies' mocking taunt that he was 'King of the Jews'. But when applied to Christ these very human ideas of kingship are turned upside down: what the title 'Christ the King' in fact expresses is his humility.

For Christ, although he is in the form of God, did not think it robbery to assume the form of a servant; although he is the transcendent, eternal, immutable God, he emptied himself and descended, to become a temporal, mutable human being; although all honour, glory and worship are due to him, he humbled himself to become man, a carpenter's son, to render loving obedience and service to God the Father, trusting and hoping in him even to death.

In other words, as in all other aspects of his human life, Christ is a model and inspiration to us of what a truly human life, lived in relation to God, should and must be – humility exalts; pride casts down.

Christ's life, death and resurrection teach us that humble dependence, trust, obedience, love and service will ultimately lift us up to God; that pride and self-regard will cast us down: kingship is humble service, not lordship of an earthly kingdom of rule and domination. Pilate need not have feared.

This subversive truth – that kingship is service – is often borne out by those human beings who seem to hold the most distinguished roles, but who are often also distinguished by their humility. They hold positions or jobs that they have not sought, but that they have been called to. They are not comfortable, easy, peaceful jobs but challenging, exhausting, self-sacrificing jobs, taken on, in obedience, trust and hope, in response to God's call, by those who tend to feel unworthy of them. I'm thinking of Mary, the queen of heaven, at the annunciation, who submitted her will to God's will and dedicated her body to his service; of our own queen, who has dedicated her life to service of others, with a strong sense of vocation and duty; I'm also thinking, in my more immediate context, of my colleagues.

In the Italian Dolomites there is a wonderful twelfth-century collegiate church with a raised altar. Suspended high up in the centre is a group of carved, wooden figures: the crucified Christ, with his mother Mary and the apostle John on either side. This Christ was not a Christ in agony, twisted and distorted by suffering, but a calm, serene, crowned King – a king with arms outstretched, nailed to a cross, looking down compassionately, piercingly, on those below him. Humility exalts; pride casts down.

So the answer to the relation between Jesus of Nazareth and Christ the King is that kingship is service; that human life is one of humble obedience to God, who turns our human pride on its head and subverts it by becoming man; that humility exalts and pride casts down.

Remembrance: but why?

Nigel Biggar

Remembrance Sunday marks the eleventh hour of the eleventh day of the eleventh month – the moment when the guns fell silent on the Western Front in 1918 and the Armistice ending World War One came into effect. Ever since, Remembrance ceremonies have been held in Britain and the Commonwealth either on 11 November or on the nearest Sunday, or on both.

But what exactly are such ceremonies *for*? What *is* it that we gather to remember, and *how* do we remember it? The truth is that on Remembrance Sunday we do a variety of things. What's more, different people do different, sometimes even contradictory, things. Indeed, sometimes it feels as if the contradiction runs not only between us, but through us. For Remembrance Sunday conjures up a gaggle of emotions, which can embarrass and confuse us.

Let's see if we can throw some light on the confusion.

Some people feel that Remembrance ceremonies are by their very nature militaristic, and are therefore unchristian, and should be avoided. This seems most plausible when church services involve military personnel in uniform and carrying flags. My own view is that not everything military is militaristic. One can carry a flag without waving it. The Remembrance Day ceremony at the Cenotaph in Westminster, notwithstanding its bemedalled veterans, its military bands and its regimental flags, does not foster a jingoistic mood, but a sombre one. Remembrance ceremonies – or Remembrance Sunday services – need not be militaristic, and I don't think that Christians need to feel embarrassed by them on that count. We needn't feel contradiction or tension running right through us at this point.

This is all the more so when we observe that one of the main things that we remember on Remembrance Sunday are the evils of war. We remember the dead. We remember young lives cut short. We remember *very* young lives cut short. If you visit military cemeteries of the two world wars the most striking, even shocking, thing is the age of those who were killed – 18, 19, 20, 21. And then, in addition to the dead, are the more numerous wounded, and the even more numerous bereaved.

War causes great damage, great loss, great evil. And it's important for us to remember that, so we don't take for granted the peace that we now enjoy. My grandparents suffered two world wars; my parents suffered one. I have suffered none. For me, peace is normal. Wars, if they happen, happen elsewhere. But that hasn't always been the case, and we ought not to assume that it *will* always be the case. Peace is fragile. It needs our active care and attention; it needs our work. And remembering the evils of war reminds us of that. So this kind of remembrance is salutary. It is pacific. It makes for peace.

So far, I think I can presume that we are agreed. So far, I doubt that there is difference between us. But when it comes to the issue of war as an instrument of justice, I imagine that we – both as a body of citizens and as a body of Christians – will find ourselves disagreeing. After all, on this matter, we in the Church always have disagreed.

The *Deutscher Soldatenfriedhof* – the German military cemetery – at Maleme in Crete is where the decisive battle was fought in May 1941 between British, Australian, New Zealand and Greek troops on the one hand, and German paratroops on the other. At the cemetery, there is a very well-presented exhibition, part of which tells the story of three brothers. All three were in the same German parachute regiment. The two younger brothers, who hero-worshipped the older one, had followed him into his elite regiment. All three of them were killed on the same day at Maleme; the youngest one was still in his teens. A very tragic story. And from this story, and others like it, the exhibition at Maleme draws the conclusion: war is evil, and we must resolve to avoid it absolutely and everywhere.

At this point in the exhibition, I found myself becoming stereotypically British, and rather un-European, in my reaction. I thought to myself, 'Well, yes ... but no', because one thing that the exhibition didn't touch on – one thing it was disingenuously silent about – was the awkward question of what young Germans were doing dropping out of the skies on to Crete in May 1941. And that then raises the sharp question of how those on the ground were supposed to respond to them. The only way to have avoided war at all costs would have been to allow Hitler's armies to do as they wished. And if in Crete, then also throughout Europe. But with what consequences – for Jews, for Slavs, for communists, for gays, for gypsies and, indeed, for non-Fascist Christians?

It's true that some Christians think that non-violent resistance, such as was effective against the British in India, could have been used successfully against the Nazis in Europe, but I, for one, remain sceptical.

If you should happen to share my scepticism, then you will entertain the possibility that war, with all its undoubted and great evils, might still be the only effective way of stopping even greater evils. War as an instrument, a terrible instrument, of justice. War as an instrument so terrible that we should seek to avoid it at great cost – but not at all costs.

'Fine,' people may say, 'perhaps the war against Hitler was justified; and so we can remember those Irishmen who served and suffered in the Allied cause with pride and gratitude. But what about World War One – surely that was a futile war, an imperialist war whose motives and aims had no moral justification? How can we remember that with anything but embarrassment and shame?'

Well, embarrassment and shame have their place on an occasion like this. Even justified wars have their shameful moments: the war against Hitler had its bombing of Dresden. So perhaps we should mingle pride with shame. But to mingle is not to eclipse. Maybe loyalty to the truth of the matter requires that we learn to live with the tension of both.

But before we buy into the debunking view of World War One that has reigned since the era of Vietnam, there are three points to consider on behalf of the justice of the Allied cause. First, to observe that that cause involved imperial interests is, to my mind, not to say anything very illuminating. There are empires and there are empires. And some empires, like nations, churches and individuals, have mixed moral records. The British empire, for example, occasioned the brutal rampages of the Black and Tans in 1920s Ireland; but 18 years later that same empire offered the only effective opposition to the Fascist domination of Europe in 1939–41. And if the British empire did give rise at times to disgusting racist contempt, it was also the first institution to abolish the slave trade and the institution of slavery, and to enforce the ban internationally. Whatever Britain's imperial interests in World War One, British troops would not have found themselves at Gallipoli and the Somme had not the Kaiser's Germany, unprovoked, invaded Belgium and France in 1914.

Second, it is common nowadays, as mentioned above, to refer to World War One as 'futile' – meaning that it achieved nothing worthwhile – but that's not how most of those involved saw it. At the time most people believed it was necessary to fend off aggressive, Prussian militarism. Even the famous war poets wrote of the piteousness of war, but not of its futility. True, Siegfried Sassoon protested that it should be stopped, but not because it should never have been started. Instead, he believed that it was being prolonged unnecessarily – although that was a view he later recanted. To most of those at the time, World War One was terrible, tragic, piteous, heartbreaking – but necessary. And that, as far as I can judge, is also the view that now prevails among contemporary historians.

But surely, people say, *nothing* could have been worth all that slaughter? Well, that raises an important and difficult question: how much is justice worth? When are its costs too high? And that brings us to a third point we have to bear in mind: the average daily rate of fatal casualties suffered by the British at the Somme in 1916 was *less* than that suffered by the British in Normandy in 1944. Normandy was more costly in human lives, per average day, than the Somme. The reason that World War One *looks* so excessively expensive in terms of lives lost is because in World War Two, Britain never fought in the main theatre of action, and it was the Russians who bore most of the costs. So if we believe that the war against Hitler was somehow 'worth it', despite its enormous overall cost – some 62 million are reckoned to have died – then the terrible number of British casualties of World War One does not, alone, prove it unjustified.

All of this excursus into World War One is a way of saying that it is not clear to me that those who lost their lives for the Allied cause between 1914 and 1918 wasted them. It's not clear that either the cause or its instrument were unjust. So maybe a measure of pride and gratitude can enter into our remembering.

Together we remember and lament the terrible evils of war. Together we remember and lament the tragedy that envelops people on all sides in wartime. Together we remember and lament the fragility of peace. And out of our remembering and lamenting, together we resolve to *work* for the peace that is only ever an achievement, never a natural, default state.

Beyond this, we divide. Some, having drawn pacifist conclusions, will resolve to oppose all war everywhere. Others of us, believing that war can sometimes be an instrument of justice, will be proud of those who have served and suffered justly, and grateful to them. But, remembering that war is only ever a *terrible* instrument of justice, which brings great evils in its wake, we will resolve to use it very sparingly indeed, and only as a very last resort.

Nevertheless, those of us who believe in the possibility of justified war will recognize that there are two temptations, not just one. Certainly, there is the temptation for nations that possess military hammers to presume that all problems are nails. Such nations would be pre-eminently the USA and, to a much lesser extent, the UK. But there is another temptation that faces most European nations that, possessing no military hammer, are prone to pretend that nails don't exist. It is possible to go to war too late, as well as too soon. For example, in 1999 during a debate on NATO's military intervention in Kosovo at the General Synod of the Church of England, the then Bishop of Oxford, Richard Harries, said this: 'Terrible things happened earlier, especially [the massacre of 7,000 Muslim men and boys at Srebrenica] in Bosnia. Should we have intervened earlier at that point? If we did not intervene at that point and should have done, how much responsibility do [we] bear for failing to face up to evil and [to] support the necessary stern measures?'

And, of course, in Rwanda we didn't go to war at all – which was good for us, but not so good for the Tutsis.

So, in addition to remembering and lamenting, and resolving to work for peace and resisting going to war too soon, some of us will also pray – on behalf of ourselves, of our fellow citizens, and above all of those to whom we have delegated the awful burdens of national leadership – for the courage not to go to war too late, and for the wisdom to discern when the moment for action has come.

On Remembrance Sunday, then, we're doing a variety of things. Some of them we do together; some we do apart. But every one of us, I think, has sufficient reason why, at the going down of the sun, and in the morning, we *should* remember them.

Story

In the Beginning, the Word

MARTYN PERCY[27]

In the beginning was the Word. And the Word was with God, and the Word was God. He was with God in the Beginning. Through him all things were made; without him nothing was made that has been made. In him was life, and that life was the light for all creation. The light shines in the darkness, but the darkness does not comprehend it.

When he awoke from the dark he did not know where he was. All was strange. He could barely see, barely sense, barely touch. But he was conscious. Even if it was a dream, he was still there: alive. He had being.

He became aware of figures, moving. Of noise, smells and of presence – all different to what he had known. An oil lamp sat near his head. It was not the only light but it was the only one he noticed and he instinctively turned his head towards it. Even though he could not make it out or focus, it was a kind of gentle warmth to him.

He had little sense of what he was wearing and what he was lying on. All he knew was that he couldn't move: he was paralysed. Not because he was immobile, but because he was bound in cloths from head to foot. But he didn't feel afraid; he didn't struggle. He felt safe, as he lay there in the hinterland between dreams and the cold air that surrounded him.

Home had been familiar. Now he was no longer there, but here; he knew that, he thought. This place was so cold and un-familiar. For a start it smelt – lots of smells, mixed together and never experienced before. And the noises. God, the noises: moans, groans, rustling, chattering, crunching, sucking and slurping – some very close; others distant and calm. He tried to raise his hands in defence or in defiance, but being bound he could not. He began to fear as he craved for the place that had once been all his.

He could not speak, and movement was impossible. So he began to open his mouth and a scream came out. He didn't know why. Loneliness? Anger? Fear? Hunger? Ah, yes, that was it: hunger. No sooner had he let out a cry than he had felt his empty stomach for the first time that day. It ached for food. Hunger was new to him. Food came. It was a drink, warm and sweet: he drank greedily, barely pausing for breath as he gulped.

Someone or something was feeding him; even in this half-light, there was now a familiar presence. Contentment spread throughout his body like the thawing of a frost on a sunny spring day. He fell into a state of peace and then into the land of sleep. And then he dreamed. It would be his last dream for a long time. In his dream he danced.

There were two others, a man and a woman, and they held hands lightly as they whirled around together on a huge, lush grassy lawn. They were overlooked by a beautiful and enormous mansion, with so many rooms, their windows smiling in the light. So much dancing, so many happy sounds came from that house as they danced together, whirling around and around, laughing into each other's eyes and enjoying the fullness of their love. They sang as they played together:

> We three, we three
> put the apple back
> on to the tree.
> See through this dance
> All shall be free.

In that land, in that dream, everything was so big, so lovely, so overflowing. Nothing ever ended; the house seemed to go on for ever, the music never stopped and the laughter seemed to expand and fill all space and then go even beyond that. It was a ceaseless place. But then the dream began to fade. The sights dimmed and the music faded to a distant echo and then disappeared. Tiredness and loss returned, the numbing feeling of displacement and the thought that all sensation is illusion. He was alone. He would never dream that dream again: lost, for ever.

When he awoke, it was with a start. Still bound head to foot, still the same unfamiliar smells and sounds. Everything was so open, so exposed, so cold. And now so uncomfortable, so he began to cry. He was lying in dirt and was wet. It was his own wetness and his own filth: once warm and pleasant to feel, it was now cold to the skin. Again he listened – he could see so little. Figures were shadows, the oil lamp a fuzzy glow. He began to cry again, this time for comfort. Deep coughing sobs welled up from within him. He was so empty, so empty, just like this place. In no time, someone or something came. He was unbound, then washed, then held, then fed. Another drink, warm and sweet. Peace returned, and he fell back once again into semi-consciousness.

Where he now was could not have been more different from where he had come from. The place of freedom, the place of peace, the dark sea that had borne him and sustained him for what seemed like eternity was all to him. In it he had bathed and slept and known. And then one day there had been a cry, shrill and pained. The earth shook, the walls began to buckle and the ground began to open up. Then the sea had gone, drained away and lost.

A new journey had begun, a journey of flight, yet of hope. He had fallen. Fallen into the ground and into crags, teeming with life and tears. And then he had been washed up on the shore. He was found by the princess (not yet a queen) almost immediately. She knew he was coming, you see, from the dark sea. She had been waiting for months on the shore.

When he had come, he was naked except for one thing. In his hand he held a hazelnut. Some claimed it was a lucky charm. Others said it was a message from a distant land, as yet unknown. She did not know what it meant, and he just clutched it tightly and that was that. Later, when he was older, he thought his father had given it to him, but he could not recall. When you are young, everything you imagine is real.

In that place where he now lay, spiders in rafters discerned a water-walker. Swallows in nests watched for a hatchling of their own kind; sheep bleated that this lamb must be human; cows, that this calf was the last sacrifice. The star that hung in the night pierced the darkness, and spoke of the day to come.

He was in the world, and though the world was made through him, the world failed to recognize him. He came to that which was his own, but his own did not receive him. Yet to all who did receive him, he made them children like himself, children of God. The Word became flesh and dwelt among us. We have seen his glory, the glory of the child who came from above and was born below, full of grace and truth, and of dreams ...

(The idea for this narrative is indebted to two sources. The first and most obvious is Julian of Norwich, and especially her 'Shewing' of the hazelnut in the hand of God, and its meaning. The second source I wish to acknowledge is the poet Les Murray and his work entitled 'Animal Nativity', which appears in his book *Translations from the Natural World*.[28])

Part 3

Sermons and Homilies for Other Occasions

The twilight zone

Graham Ward

The Twilight Zone was first broadcast by the American TV Channel CBS in 1959. It ran for five series before being revived in the 1980s. It's now cult viewing among discerning students, with most episodes available on YouTube. For anyone like me, who remembers begging to stay up to watch it, its jarring, psychotic opening music instinctively sends shivers of delight down the spine. And its famous opening voice-over has lost nothing of its original power: 'It is a dimension as vast as space and as timeless as infinity. It is the middle ground between light and shadow, between science and superstition, and it lies between the pit of man's fears and the summit of his knowledge. This is the dimension of imagination. It is an area which we call the *Twilight Zone*.' In many ways the series was counter-cultural. The postwar West was dominated by the promises and progresses of the sciences: mechanism and empiricism paved the way to a bright future with their sophisticated bombs and their space explorations. It was underpinned, philosophically, by logical positivism: facts with the stark brutality of rocks. But the series pointed to folds in human comprehension that certain lights and times and spaces afford.

Twilight has always been a time for hauntings and stalkings; a time when the pits of human fears are stirred and hair is raised on the back of the neck. Transitional times between light and dark, at dusk and just prior to dawn, are evocative. They colour moods, as they get inside us, altering wave-lengths in the brain and endocrinal discharges. Transitional spaces do the same, which is why in every civilization known superstitions intensify around thresholds. To cross a threshold or to have one's own threshold crossed effects transformations: the stranger becomes the guest. There's a famous cult vampire novel by the Swedish writer John Lindqvist called *Let the Right One In*,[29] set in a housing estate in the suburbs of Stockholm that begins when a 12-year-old boy (Oskar) opens the door to a new, moody and mysterious neighbour. Even crossing the threshold of a church or cathedral affects posture, voice and low-lying feelings. Relationships to things change as light levels and spatial dimensions change, certainties meet unfamiliarities; in German the *heimelig* (homely) becomes the *Unheimlich* (the uncanny).

Levels of attention and alertness are heightened in these liminal times and spaces. By ancient tradition, religions have marked the temporal transitions by prayer. In the Christian Church these became liturgies like vespers, compline, matins, and the noonday angelus. In twilight zones, temporal and spatial, prayer intensifies as human beings experience subtle vulnerabilities and changes in their circadian rhythms. And the registration of such transitions and transformation is evidently longstanding, reaching far back into time as the story of Jacob wrestling with God or an angel of God reveals. This narrative of Genesis 32 is peculiar indeed. Its strange, imaginative force, its mythic resonance, has been felt over centuries by many artists: Rembrandt, Doré, Gauguin, Rilke, Dickinson, Hesse and U2's song 'Bullet the Blue Sky' from their 1987 album *The Joshua Tree*. Resonances from the scriptural story ripple through the imaginations of novelists, painters, poets, sculptors and songwriters, because it's a story from the twilight zone; a story about what happens in the twilight zone.

Thresholds are marked quite clearly: Jacob on one side of the River Jabbok, and all his family, goods and livelihood sent ahead across the river, on the other side; his old life behind him and a new, uncertain future with his estranged brother Esau ahead of him; past and future. He stands alone where the darkness gathers in a place called Penuel – which in Hebrew means 'face' – and without reason or introduction, as soon as he is alone he is abruptly wrestling a man until daybreak. The threshold marks a crossroads and a crisis. It's a place of struggle which means, spiritually, a place where prayer intensifies. It's a place of fear and profound uncertainty; a place where Jacob will either continue to live or meet his death.

The threshold is an existential edge where a human being encounters the divine beyond any deciding or polite conversation, confession of sin or appeals to righteousness. Genesis 32.25 is one of the deepest, darkest and most ambivalent lines in Holy Scripture because we are completely unsure who the 'he' refers to until the final clause: 'And when the man saw that he did not prevail against Jacob, he struck him on the hip socket'. There is total confusion here as to who is being touched, and who is doing the touching, until finally we are told, 'and *Jacob*'s [my italics] hip was put out of joint'. Verse 26 states, 'Then he [God] said, "Let me go, for the day is breaking".' Even then, wounded by God, Jacob persists, 'I will not let you go, unless you bless me.'

In the confusion and physical turmoil of being on the edge, Jacob knows only one thing: unless God bless him and establish a relationship with him, with responsibility for him, he will die. He has come to the place of having nothing – no past or future, no family or goods – so God is either with him and for him or Jacob lies down without hope, in his isolation at the threshold, and surrenders. This is the power of thresholds in the twilight zone. And when God blesses Jacob he does so by taking away the one thing that remains: his name. In Hebrew thought to have no name is not to participate in the orders of creation, that's why Adam must name all that God brings before him on the day of his own creation. But at the point where even his name is taken from him, Jacob is given a new name, Israel, which means a prince of God. He now passes on, the sun rising behind him, limping towards a new understanding of who he is. His time in the twilight zone is a walk through the valley of the shadow of death.

What he *is* now he is not sure; what he is certain of is his encounter with God. What he *has* now is God with him, but it has cost him everything, and he remains to his death affected by the limp, a reminder that all Israel will remember after him not to eat that part of an animal's body (Genesis 32.31–32).

Jacob's story is a tale from the twilight zone – profoundly resonant with a significance that cannot be pinned down, as any encounter with God cannot be pinned down. The meaning of the encounter escapes us. We only know we have been encountered. There is some small analogy here with coming to the altar to receive Christ in the Eucharist. Here at the altar-rail is a Jabbok moment. So what will you or I receive, and what will you or I have to give that we might receive? Jacob passes his testimony down to the Israelites: 'For I have seen God face to face, and yet my life is preserved' (Genesis 32.30).

The Angel of the Lord and Gideon

Martyn Percy

I am going to begin with this beautiful meditation from Bishop David Walker, called simply 'An Angelic Salutation':

> For a long while they sat opposite each other, gently holding hands. She with her head bent, her body racked with sobs; the Angel calm, still, waiting for the word that would have to be spoken. At last the woman lifted her head, pushed her hair away from tear-stained cheeks, and said, simply, 'I can't'. Silence followed. She was gathering her energies to offer a reason, a rationale for why her courage had failed her; why she, who had always been obedient to God's will and law, was now with-holding her consent. 'Don't be afraid', said the Angel. He'd used those words before, at the very beginning of the meeting, when his sudden presence, and the light that quietly emanated from him, had so clearly scared her. Now half-formed sentences began to tumble from her: about her place within this close-knit community; the shame that the inevitable gossip and accusa-tions would bring both on her and her family; the loneliness of a life as a tainted woman, one no man would take as wife; the pull towards prostitution, in the struggle to sustain herself and the child she would bear. It was too much. Please let this cup pass from her.

The Angel still held on to her as tightly as ever. Only when she had emptied herself of both her words and her tears did he respond. 'Fear not', he said, for a third time. 'God loves you. He loves you as deeply as ever. This was never a command, always an invitation to come on a particular journey with him. Go in peace. Marry. Have children, and bring them up in that same love of the Lord which you yourself know. And teach them this; that God, in their generation, will do this great thing. Tell them to be alert, to watch for the signs that the Promised One is coming among them. Live long, do not regret your decision today; but of your mercy, when you hear of Him, pray for His mother.'

He stood up, passed out of the house, walked perhaps a stone's throw away from the building, then stopped to wipe a hand across his eyes. He gazed back at the woman's home for some minutes. Silently, he held her and all that she was before the One who had sent him. From somewhere within his robes he pulled out a scroll and unfurled it. It was a list of names, women's names. Many had already been crossed through, and now there was another to strike out. He looked at the details for his next assignment. Another unpromising village, another pious but conventional upbringing. Another dispiritingly traditional name. Mary.[30]

The encounter that Gideon has with an angel in Judges 6.11–23 is one of the best-loved stories of the Old Testament. Gideon belongs to the tribe of Israel – but to one of the weakest clans. Moreover, for the last seven years, the Israelites have been oppressed by the Midianites. Actually, more than oppressed. They have been economically savaged. The Midianites take everything – crops, sheep, goats, cattle, and all the food the Israelites grow. The Israelites are reduced to growing crops in secret. The Midianites feed off the Israelites, says the text, *like locusts*.

There are exact parallels with the 1998 Pixar film *A Bug's Life*. In the film, a bunch of grasshoppers come every year to the anthill, and eat what the ants have gathered for themselves. The 'offering', as the ants call the ritual, is a part of their fate. Flik – the lead bug– sets off to find bugs that are willing to fight the grasshoppers but nobody expects him to succeed. And due to a misunderstanding, Flik returns with a circus crew who are announced as the agents of redemption that everybody longs for. It is about as absurd as Gideon taking on the Midianites with his friends.

A Bug's Life is a retelling of Aesop's fable *The Ant and the Grass-hopper*, and Akira Kurosawa's 1954 film *Seven Samurai*, in which seven masterless Samurai save villagers from rampant exploit-ation at the hands of marauding bandits. A later Americanized version of this film appeared as *The Magnificent Seven*, with exploited Mexican peasants now playing the role of economically ravaged Japanese villagers. That the Israelites are 'ant-like' should not surprise us. The Book of Judges goes out of its way to stress Gideon's resourcefulness – he's threshing wheat in a winepress; hard, secretive work that he has to do for his people, as well as serve his oppressors.

Marauding bandits, it seems, are the same the world over. You just need a small ant to save the day. Or a small guy called Gideon who, somewhat laughably, is referred to as a 'mighty warrior' by the angel. Gideon is no fool, though, and he is not easily flattered either. So when the angel tells Gideon that they are going to fight the Midianites and win, Gideon is understandably sceptical. His reasoned reply to God can be summarized as follows: 'when it comes to fighting I'm pretty crap (but I can cook a decent stew). And we are in a crap situation with crap resources, living in a crap time. But you say we are on the point of victory. That must be more crap, God. But no offence meant.'

None taken, it would seem. The angel knows that the scepticism of Gideon would be deep and rational; and it is well-founded. We should not underestimate the absurdity of the promise to Gideon. So, not unreasonably, he asks for signs from God. The reason being, I think, that he does not want to raise false hopes. The signs he asks for are not about his lack of faith – though I expect he was sceptical to the core – but rather his responsibility and fidelity to his desperate people.

The Old Testament is not only full of people demanding signs; it is also full of the strange signs by which God speaks to us. The irony should not be lost on us. A burning bush; a rock that flows with water; a pillar of flame; or even a talking ass – God can speak through all these things. But the actual sign is often not the point. A religion that regularly gathered around the hind quarters of a beast of burden, hoping to hear the Oracles of God, would be a very odd faith. So would cooking a stew and expecting a message from God in the ensuing instant flambé; or one of Gideon's fleeces to say a word or two.

In *Angels on Command*, a book by Larry Keefauver,[31] the author writes that 'God sent an angel to tell a nobody that he was indeed somebody in God's sight'. God does that. God uses those who are small in their own eyes to do great things. Keefauver also writes that the story can encourage anyone to derive their confidence from 'choosing to see themselves as God sees them': Gideon saw himself as weak and helpless. But the angel declared God's perspective on Gideon: 'O mighty man of valour' (Judges 6.12). So, we are challenged to see ourselves as God sees us. The invitation is to simply let go of those insecurities that often keep us from enjoying the fullness of God's hopes for our lives. God sometimes commands his angels to lift us up: to propel us above poor self-imagery or other circumstances that conspire to grip and shape our thinking.

There is a connection with Paul's words in 1 Corinthians 1.20–31 and Judges 6. Jews demand signs; Greeks demand wisdom. But no sign was to be given in the New Testament, except the sign of the cross – foolishness to the Greeks, and stumbling block to us all. The love of God, says one hymn writer, is broader than the measure of our mind. So it is with wisdom, which is why God uses simple things to shame the intelligent, and the foolish to confound the wise. God's messages often come through unexpected sources. He even chose to reveal the Word made flesh through a baby – who could not speak, at least to begin with. God's wisdom is not like ours; it surprises, undermines and confounds. It does not confirm; it often disturbs.

One of the reasons why the stories of the Old Testament are so likeable is that the characters are all quite flawed: the good, the bad and the ugly are all mixed up. And frequently, the resolution and salvation for individuals is to let go and let God. Think of Jonah on his sulky journey to Nineveh, or any of the other prophets who come and go. Even Gideon is pretty hopeless.

But what of Gideon's angel? Well, sometimes the messenger is the message. We don't have a physical description of the angel, but what we do know is that the angel was prepared to be tested by Gideon. And tested until Gideon could be reasonably sure that the near suicide mission he was being asked to embark upon might have a sliver of a chance of succeeding. Gideon was being invited to pitch his pathetic compatriots against the combined forces of the Amorites, Midianites and Amelekites. He wanted to be sure that the angel was truly a messenger from God, and not simply a hopeless optimist. The angel obliges Gideon on each of his tests – the so-called 'fleece test' being the last. But Gideon still has to commit his puny forces against the might of his enemies. And at the risk of a cliché, to do this he has to set aside his fear, and step out in faith. The message and messenger all say the same; we can haggle with God, but we can't hide. The angel is God's negotiator, closing the deal.

Yet it's only when Gideon lets go of the negotiations and stops testing God with signs that he begins to experience the blessing of God. But a blessing can be a shocking revelation. Indeed, it can turn your world upside down.

It is commonplace, sometimes, to believe that when we encounter suffering or abandonment that we have somehow failed God, or incurred his wrath. So that when we cry out for healing and deliverance, we are asking God to remove some pain or suffering that he has somehow permitted, or perhaps even bestowed. Surely, we reason, that if we had been really good, we would not really be suffering?

It is a fact that Jesus nowhere explains the origins of suffering. He heals; he consoles; he weeps; he loves. But he is not a philosopher who explains why bad things happen to good people. He does not at any point explain the origin of evil or the ultimate source of pain and suffering. What Jesus does do, however, is live and echo the psalms. He is the good shepherd. He is with us in the valley of the shadow. He does not abandon us in our pain, desolation and suffering. He walks with us. He hears us when we cry out. God cannot forget us. God does not know how to be absent.

And when we are lifted out of the darkness, we find that God has something else for us. It reminds me of a story Terry Waite tells of his imprisonment under Hezbollah in Lebanon. Moved from place to place to avoid detection, and frequently blindfolded and bound, he found himself one day bundled into the boot of a car. As he was being driven along, he sensed in the darkness another person, also bound and blindfolded. It was John McCarthy. 'There's not much room in this boot', quipped Terry. 'There was a lot more until you got in', replied John. They were to spend years in captivity. But what sustained them, partly, were the ancient hymns, collects and prayers of the Church that they had committed to memory. And the knowledge, that no matter how alone they felt, they were neither abandoned nor forgotten by God – and indeed all God's people, continually praying for them. It is this that now drives Terry's work for the homeless. Just as he was once deprived of home and humanity during his captivity in Lebanon, he now works for the homeless and rootless in our own society.

The angel comes to Gideon in Israel's darkest hour with a message of deliverance. But the angel confounds our wisdom at the same time. Gideon, who thought he was just a weakling, is now to be called 'mighty one'. Perhaps just like the angel that spoke to a peasant girl called Mary 2,000 years ago, and called her 'favoured one', when she clearly wasn't. Both Gideon and Mary, however, have to respond to God's invitation – no matter how unwise this might look if you start to rationalize it – to become a mighty warrior or a favoured peasant girl. Perhaps God's angel speaks to you and me, here and now. The angels all seem to say the same thing in the midst of our darkest hour: 'I have something quite extraordinary for you to do; but don't be afraid, for the Lord is with you.'

Martyrs

Martyn Percy

A fragrant offering and sacrifice

> Herod feared John, knowing that he was a righteous and holy
> man, and he protected him. When he [Herod] heard him, he was
> greatly perplexed; and yet he liked to listen to him ... [Eventu-
> ally] the king sent a soldier of the guard with orders to bring
> John's head. He went and beheaded him in the prison, brought
> his head on a platter ... When [John's] disciples heard about
> it, they came and took his body, and laid it in a tomb. (Mark
> 6.20–29)

John the Baptist was something of a rebel. In one sense we could
regard him as a kind of zealot in the Castro tradition, or even
perhaps a 'religious Che Guevara'. He seems to almost wilfully
court trouble, and his religious zeal and idealism tip him deep
into the politics of his day. He doesn't just baptize people who
seek him out. He's out there, calling people to repent – and he is
unafraid to speak this message to the top echelons of society, as
much as he is unafraid to risk the wrath of the masses to whom
he also preaches. In modern idiom, we might say John was a bit
of a crusader. Indeed, there is a sense of the *jihad* in him. Now
here I don't imply, of course, any violence on his part. There was
none. But as classical and modern Islamic scholars say, the Koran
affirms that the truest and best jihad is of the pen. We engage with
and defeat our enemies not by a war or violence, but by dialogue
and persuasion.

Of course if we were to call John the Baptist 'Jihadi John',
it would be to conflate with an image and memory of extreme
terror. Mohammed Emwazi was a British man who was thought
to be the person seen in several videos produced by the Islamic
extremist group ISIL showing the beheadings of a number of
captives in 2014 and 2015. Just like the theatre of Jihadi John's
videoed executions, John the Baptist has his head brought into a
feast on a platter. Why beheading? What is it about this kind of
killing or execution that we find so dreadful? Well, first a word

about terror. Consider this account, for example, of the death of Polycarp from the early *Acts of the Christian Martyrs* (AD 155):

> the men in charge of the fire started to light it. A great flame blazed up and those of us to whom it was given to see beheld a miracle ... for the flames, bellying out like a ship's sail in the wind, formed into the shape of a vault and thus surrounded the martyr's body as with a wall. And he was within it not as burning flesh, but rather as bread being baked, or like gold and silver being purified in a smelting furnace. And from it we perceived such a delightful fragrance as though it were smoking incense or some other costly perfume ...[32]

Christianity is a faith of the senses. There are things of beauty to see and texts to read; sounds and words to hear; artefacts and objects to touch; and sacraments to taste and savour. But we rarely think of our faith in terms of its sense of smell. But this is all rather surprising when one considers just how important the olfactory imagination is in the ancient world: 'the scent of salvation', to borrow a phrase from the theologian Susan Ashbrook Harvey. For in the scents, smells and odours of Scripture, tradition and Church, we have intimations of the divine. As one anthropologist, Clifford Geertz, says, 'religious symbols *reek* of meaning'.[33] And sometimes they literally do reek – the message is in the scent.

In the account of the martyrdom of Polycarp, we are introduced to the resonances between scent and meaning: the aroma of baking bread is a eucharistic hint, and the smell of gold or silver being purified is a promise for believers. Here, in Polycarp's death, we have the hint of salvation and eternal life for all believers. The early Christians were also keenly in touch with the senses of smell and taste, and their links with worship and the presence of God. Christ is both bread and wine; to taste and see is to enter into communion. This is not just cerebral; it is also sensual. Manna in the wilderness, or sweet water in the desert, are tokens of both comfort and abiding nourishment. Ephesians 5 tells us 'to walk in love, as Christ loved us and gave himself for us – a fragrant offering and sacrifice to God'. In 2 Corinthians 2.14–16 Paul writes:

'But thanks be to God, who in Christ ... and through us spreads in every place the *fragrance* [my italics] that comes from knowing him.'

The Carthusian Martyrs of London were the monks of the London Charterhouse, the monastery of the Carthusian Order in central London, and who were put to death by the English state between 1535 and 1537. The method of execution was hanging, removal of genitals, disembowelling while still alive, beheading, and then quartering. The quarters were boiled in hot water, and the severed head displayed as a trophy of the state, and as a warning to others. The death toll was 18 men, all of whom have been recognized as true martyrs.

As the literal meaning of the word indicates, 'terror' is a military strategy that hopes to change the political situation by spreading fear rather than by causing enormous material damage. Every military action spreads fear. But in conventional warfare, fear is a *by-product* of material losses. In terrorism or dictatorship, fear is the whole story, and there is an astounding disproportion between the actual strength of the terrorists or dictators, and the fear they manage to inspire.

Second, there is also something symbolic about hanging, beheading, disembowelling and quartering. This is about dis-membering. We know from Scripture that faces – our face, and the face of God – are how we are known, recognized, and ultimately cherished. To remove the head is to remove a person's identity – to literally erase someone. And that word – erase – means literally 'to scrape off, shave; abolish, remove'. A hanging throttles the voice; a beheading cuts through the neck and the throat, terminating the breath and speech; it renders the mouth apart from the body. The neck is one of the most vulnerable parts of the human body. Rendered asunder, no feeding and no breathing means there will be no more life. This person will not speak again; erased, their body now becomes anonymous – a mere nothing.

Third, we can begin to see why, perhaps, the beheadings are not just part of terrorism – whether by groups or by movements – but also part of a nation or state's weaponry. In Nanjing, China, at the Museum of the Holocaust, the Chinese people commemorate the thousands of their citizens dismembered by the conquering

Japanese forces in World War Two. The Nazis executed thousands of prisoners by beheading. Perhaps surprisingly, France
only banned beheading in 1981. It was the only legal means of
capital punishment in France from 1789 until the end of the twentieth century.

Beheading, then, even in the hands of the state, is vindictive; it
is a statement of triumph; of total victory; of annihilation. It is the
destruction and humiliation of a body: 'his [John's] disciples ...
came and took his body, they laid it in a tomb' (Mark 6.29). No
further explanation is needed. But there is a real tenderness and
some pragmatism here. You see the shadows of this, even in a film
such as *Love Actually* (2003), where we hear Hugh Grant open
with these words:

> Whenever I get gloomy with the state of the world, I think about
> the arrivals gate at Heathrow Airport. General opinion is start-
> ing to make out that we live in a world of hatred and greed, but
> I don't see that. It seems to me that love is everywhere. Often
> it's not particularly dignified or newsworthy, but it's always
> there – fathers and sons, mothers and daughters, husbands and
> wives, boyfriends, girlfriends, old friends. When the planes hit
> the Twin Towers, as far as I know, none of the phone calls from
> the people on board were messages of hate or revenge – they
> were all messages of love.

Martyrs live in love and die in love, so they are quite different from
suicide bombers. Suicide bombers plant seeds of hate; they take
others with them. There is collateral damage – carnage, misery,
death and destruction are all spread by their actions. But martyrs,
even in death, grow only love. They fulfill what Jesus proclaims
in John 12.24: 'Very truly, I tell you, unless a grain of wheat falls
into the earth *and* [my italics] dies, it remains just a single grain;
but if it dies, it bears much fruit.' That is why Tertullian (AD
150–240) said, 100 years after John wrote his Gospel, that 'the
blood of the martyrs is the seed of the Church'.

John the Baptist's disciples simply came and collected his body,
and carried on with the business of love and faith. The response
to the death of their beloved leader was not a hateful revenge, but
rather faithfulness and love. And so where does this place John

the Baptist? Or, for that matter, some irritant rebellious Carthusian monks or others whom the Church commemorates? They move in life, and especially in death, from being regional political and religious irritants, to being true martyrs. 'He must increase, but I must decrease' is John the Baptist's prayer (John 3.30). Martyrs live in love and die in love. Though dead, we remember that they loved to the end – and so continue to live in our hearts and histories. Enduring love is their legacy.

Witnesses – after the ascension

Sarah Foot

Ascensiontide is a short ecclesiastical season, but one in which the whole Church has to make an important transition. In the days between the Feast of the Ascension and Whit Sunday, we have to prepare to leave our Easter alleluias behind and get ready for the descent of the Holy Spirit on the disciples. That event is often described as marking the birth of the Church and the launch of its mission to the world. A little like Advent, or Holy Saturday, Ascensiontide is an interim period, lying between promise and fulfilment. In this interval we may pause and reflect while we wait upon the Lord. But it would be an error to see this merely as a transitional season, one to be hurried through as fast as possible until we reach the real business of the Church, given the power of the Spirit on the day of Pentecost. We should make space to exalt and worship the risen Christ, ascended into heaven and seated on the right hand of the Father.

In marking the ascension, we also need to pay heed to the injunctions made by Christ to his disciples before he was carried up to heaven. The first chapter of the Acts of the Apostles reports the final words that Jesus spoke to his disciples on earth, words that we should read in parallel with those put into Jesus' mouth at the end of the Gospel of Luke: 'But you will receive power when the Holy Spirit has come upon you; and you will be my witnesses in Jerusalem, in all Judea and Samaria, and to the ends of the earth' (Acts 1.8).

Geographically, Acts begins where Luke's Gospel ends: at the heart of the Jewish world in Jerusalem in the formation of the first apostolic community (a proto-church on which successive generations of Christians would later model their own collective endeavours). But the book ends far from Jerusalem, with the triumphant entry of the apostle Paul into Rome. As Paul himself said, it was 'for the sake of the hope of Israel' (Acts 28.20) that he was bound, arrested and brought to trial at the heart of the Roman empire. In the course of Luke's two-book narrative, the message of Jesus is enlarged to embrace the world of the gentiles, extending all the way 'to the ends of the earth'.

Luke had already offered a similar narrative at the end of his Gospel. After the last appearance of Jesus to his disciples, he went on to open their minds to understand the Scriptures, where – he reminded them – it is written 'that repentance and forgiveness of sins is to be proclaimed in his name to all nations, beginning from Jerusalem' (Luke 24.46–47).

Jesus' disciples, whom he thus sent out into this world, just as the Father had sent him, Christ, into the world (John 17.18), would be responsible for bringing future generations to faith. Although their ministry of spreading the gospel away from Jerusalem and the surrounding area as far, eventually, as the ends of the earth, could begin only after the coming of the Holy Spirit at Pentecost, it was Christ's last words that mandated the disciples to take the good news not just to the Jews, but also to the gentiles. In fulfilment of that commission, later generations of missionaries would draw on the teaching of the apostles to spread the faith across the lands of the former Roman empire. Ultimately the word came to a new people living at what was, then, the very edge – or corner – of the known world: the English.

The early English historian the Venerable Bede opened *History of the English Church and People*[34] by locating the British Isles within a contemporary geographical framework, one that placed Jerusalem at the heart of the known world, Rome at the centre of the Christian West, and Britain at the extreme edge. 'Britain', he said in his first sentence, is 'an island of the ocean and lies to the north-west, being opposite Germany, Gaul and Spain, which form the greater part of Europe'.[35] When he recounted the process by which the good news of salvation came to this utter-most corner of the world, and to the people dwelling there, Bede consistently used a Pauline image of conversion as freedom from slavery. Pope Gregory was supposedly inspired to send a mission to Britain because of his encounter with some English slave boys in the market in Rome. Their fair-skinned faces reminded him of angels (*angeli*) and so he sent monks from his own monastic community in Rome to preach the word of God to the *Angli*, the English race. 'We can and should by rights call Gregory our apostle', Bede wrote, 'for though he held the most important see in the whole world and was head of churches which had long been converted to the true faith, yet he made our nation, till then enslaved to idols, into a church of Christ.'[36]

Bede presented Pope Gregory's sending of missionaries to the English as a continuation of earlier apostolic missions. Gregory himself had written in his commentary on Job that 'pagans, too, are called to God and God has sent his preachers to the ends of the earth for the ministry of preaching'. But Bede, who modelled the shape of his *History of the English Church and People* on Luke's Acts, went further. He argued that the conversion of the English fulfilled Christ's injunction to his disciples that they should wit-ness to him 'in Jerusalem, in all Judea and Samaria, and to the ends of the earth' (Acts 1.8).

In pausing to mark Ascensiontide, we reflect on these links across time and space that tie our own Church's history into the very beginnings of apostolic ministry. The conversion of the *Angli* at the corner, *angulus*, of the world made the English people members of the holy universal Church of Christ, sharing in its pilgrimage on earth. Through their baptism, the English were united with the *angulus*, the cornerstone, namely with Christ him-self, and so they became incorporated into the universal house of God. That house, Bede saw as a figure both of Christ 'as the uniquely chosen and precious cornerstone laid in the foundation', and of *us* 'as the living stones, built upon the foundation of the apostles and prophets, that is upon the Lord himself'.[37]

Bede's vision of a single, unified Church was one that lay rooted in the earliest community of those who worshipped Christ as Lord and Saviour, that of the first disciples gathered together in Jerusalem. Jesus charged them to be witnesses of what they had seen and known, but his charge would be passed to many generations – of believers, disciples as yet unknown, who would tread the paths to the uttermost ends of the earth in Christ's name. Indeed Jesus imagined a line of followers stretching all the way to the end of time, all of whom would share not only in fellowship and unity with one another, but who would be one with Jesus and the Father in glory (John 17.24).

At Ascensiontide we focus on the exaltation of the risen Christ and his reception in glory; Christ's ascension was the moment when Israel's Messiah was enthroned at the right hand of God. At Ascensiontide, we yearn that we may be with him where he is, to see his glory, which the Father has given him because he loved him before the foundation of the world (John 17.24). Jesus' ascension marks a new chapter on earth in which salvation and eternal life became open to all who 'believe on the Lord Jesus'. Not just those who knew him in the flesh, but all who have confessed him crucified, risen and glorified as the Son of God. We may recall in our hearts with gratitude all those apostles who proclaimed that faith among the gentiles, especially those who brought the word to these shores. May we, like John, do so in a spirit of love and unity, so that, 'those who will believe in Christ through their word ... may all be one' (John 17.20–21).

'Hear My Prayer'

Martyn Percy

According to the American writer Anne Lamott, the prayer of the Daily Offices can be simply summarized. Morning Prayer, she suggests, can be condensed into a single word: 'whatever'. And Evening Prayer needs only two words: 'ah, well ...' Lamott says elsewhere there are only three other prayers really: 'Help', 'Thanks' and 'Wow!' We perhaps spend too much time asking, she suggests – pleading, really – and not enough time thanking. And very little time just saying of and to God, 'Wow!'

Prayer, I suppose, is one of those activities that Christians (indeed, people of all faiths) engage in, but seldom pause to consider what it is they are doing. The habitual, impromptu and mysterious nature of prayer is part of its fascination. Here we have the language of faith, of desire, of hope, of healing – and even occasionally of justification and commination. And occasionally the quirky: 'Hail, Mary, full of grace, help me find a parking space': a prayer that not only rhymes, but also seems to work – for some.

Several years ago I was an honorary chaplain to a professional rugby club. I performed all the usual duties. Perhaps inevitably, in all the fracas and fury of a game the name of God would often be invoked by the supporters. And after that crucial-but-missed-kick, my neighbour might turn to me and say, 'I don't think your boss is helping us much today.' The retort from me: 'Sorry. But I'm more sales and marketing, not production …'

In rugby, the wages of sin are a penalty. When there was a kick for goal, a prayerful hush would descend on the ground. Invariably, my fellow fans might turn to me again and exhort me to pray ('Say one for us, Padre …' – the classic request, so beloved of our vernacular spirituality). If the kick went over, I would be thanked for my successful prayers. If it missed, I'd be asked why God no longer favours the home side! And this is the heart of the matter. Most passionate sports fans *pray*. But does God intervene to answer such prayers?

If the ball goes through the posts, has my prayer been answered, or is it just coincidence? If it does not, has God declared his support for the other team? Or is it just that God doesn't care, being generally indifferent to rugby, and perhaps preferring chess, or maybe netball? So how does God act in the world? Can God affect the outcome of a rugby game? If that is possible, then should God actually do that sort of thing? Clearly, in the interests of fairness, the answer is 'no'. But that does not stop us praying for victory. So what happens when we pray? How should we pray?

Prayer is supposed to be a process whereby the petitioner is transformed, as they express their hopes and fears. In being and waiting before God, we slowly become conformed to the will and image of God. So, we do not pray for victory, but a rightful outcome. We do not pray for the kick to go over, but for the kicker to do his best. But we also remember to remind God that we will be utterly desolate and miserable if we lose. God understands that.

Not all of Jesus' prayers were answered; he too tasted the bitter chalice of defeat. And how does God return our prayerful petitions? Here are three very preliminary thoughts. First, any intervention from beyond, and by God, is often subtle and ambiguous, seldom conclusive or coercive. Second, the petitioner can never have the impossible: there is a final whistle, an ending, a result, and perhaps disappointment. It is no good praying that your team has won when the result was announced five minutes ago.

Prayer has to cope with realities, not side-step them. Anyway, sometimes there is victory. Third, the answer to our prayers is sometimes 'no'. In expressing our hopes in prayer, God may refuse us. Not because God is fickle, or supports the other team, but because there is wisdom and maturity to pursue – God does not satisfy all our desires, no matter how weighty or worthy they may seem to us.

This is why some of the great prayers we have in the English language are actually *about* prayer. They teach us to pray, as Jesus does. One thinks of Cranmer's majestic Collect for Purity: 'Almighty God, unto whom all hearts are open, all desires known, and from whom no secrets are hidden, cleanse the thoughts of our hearts ...' In other words, sift and sanctify our desires and dreams. Do not give us what we want; but do give us what we need, and what is good for us. Similarly, George Herbert comprehends the mystery of prayer – as a journey of the senses and soul, as it were – when he writes:

Prayer – the church's banquet, angel's age,
God's breath in man returning to his birth,
The soul in paraphrase, heart in pilgrimage ...
A kind of tune, which all things hear and fear;
Softness, and peace, and joy, and love, and bliss,
Exalted manna, gladness of the best,
Heaven in ordinary, man well drest,
The milky way, the bird of Paradise,
Church-bells beyond the stars heard, the soul's blood,
The land of spices; something understood.[38]

Jesus, in teaching his disciples to pray, keeps the matter simple. God will answer our prayers; he listens to persistence. But, as noted, sometimes the answer is 'no'. We are to hallow the name of God; seek the coming of his kingdom; name our needs (but *not* desires – God can *always* see what we *want* – 'no secrets are hidden', as Cranmer says); ask forgiveness for our wrongdoings; forgive others; and pray for deliverance. And in the parable of the widow and the unjust judge (Luke 18.1–8), Luke illuminates this with some additional comments.

First, God will listen to what is absorbing and consuming us. Some of these things may be obvious needs – the real hunger for food, justice, mercy and deliverance – be it ours, or that of others. And sometimes, the prayer requests may be a mix of desire and need – the kind of prayers where 'the thoughts of hearts' will need cleansing even as we petition. Yet Luke seems to be saying that God is attentive to our petitions, even when they are flawed. But even Luke has the wisdom to tell us that the prayer is answered – for example, with God giving the widow justice because of her persistence.

Indeed, Luke seems intent on encouraging us to pray persistently: to ask, knock, seek. Yet this advice is more gnomic than it at first appears. We are not told that God will answer our prayers directly, or according to our (flawed and sinful) petitions and agendas. Rather, Luke suggests that God is consistent in his attentiveness, and will always answer in love. No one who wants bread will get a stone; no one who wants a fish will get a scorpion. We need to remember what the mystics said: God does not know how to be absent. He does not know how to forget you or overlook you. He sees every sparrow that falls. He numbers the hairs of your head; he looks after one stray sheep, not just 99 compliant ones.

God can only give good things. He can only bless; he does not curse. As the rabbis say, God rules by blessing. But we need the wisdom to see what he is giving as he blesses us. Prayer, then, is attuning the soul to God's heart and mind; our wisdom finding something of an echo with the wisdom that comes from above. Mature prayer is not a shopping list to place before God. It is the self, placed before God, through which the needs and desires of the world and the individual can be set before the true light that cleanses 'the thoughts of our hearts', so that we can love and worship more perfectly.

As John Macmurray reminds us in his wonderful book *Persons in Relation*,[39] it is important to distinguish between genuine and deceptive religion. The philosophy of deceptive religion runs something like this: 'fear not; trust in God and he will see that none of the things you dread will ever happen to you'. But, says Macmurray, genuine faith and mature religion have a quite different starting point: 'fear not – the things you are most frightened of may well happen to you; but they are nothing to be afraid of'.

In the same vein, Harold Kushner in his best-selling *When Bad Things Happen to Good People*,[40] reminds us that God is not fickle. Kushner, a rabbi, dedicated this book to the memory of his young son, Aaron, who died at the age of 14 of an incurable genetic disease. So the book is written by someone who prayed hard, but whose son still died. And here are reasons people give (but that Kushner rejects) as to why you might not get what you pray for: you didn't deserve it; you didn't pray hard enough; someone more worthy was praying for the opposite result; God doesn't hear prayers.

Kushner also reminds his readers that there are improper prayers, at least according to the *Talmud*. God won't: change what already exists (e.g. the earlier result from that football game; or the sex of a baby); change the laws of nature (e.g. Origen – we cannot pray for the cool of winter in the heat of summer); let someone else be harmed; do something that is within our power so that *we* don't have to do it – like pass our law exams.

So what's left to pray for? Well, basically for deep strength and Christian character, so we can deal with adversity and reality.

And this seems to me to be partly what Jesus is driving at in the parable of the widow and the unjust judge in Luke 18. God may not bring us success or what we desire, but he does offer hope. He will reward faithfulness. In the words of Kushner: 'People who pray for courage, for strength to bear the unbearable, for the grace to remember what they have, instead of what they have lost, very often find their prayers answered ... God ... doesn't send us the problem; He gives us the strength to cope with it.'

It was Bonhoeffer who, many years ago, said God loved us enough to see Christ pushed out of the world and on to the cross. God usually meets us in weakness, compassion and love; not in absolute power. The self-limitation of God means that God meets us in love, so not in absolute power, which would only compel us. God loves us enough to give us space; he gives us space, even though are no spaces where God is not.

Most people know the so-called 'Serenity Prayer' – or at least the first part of it. Very few, however, know that the original was written by Reinhold Niebuhr in the darkest days of World War Two. The prayer goes like this:

> God, grant me grace to accept with serenity, the things that cannot be changed; courage to change the things which should be changed; and the wisdom to know the difference ... Living one day at a time, enjoying one moment at a time, accepting hardship as a pathway to peace; and taking, as Jesus did, this sinful world as it is. Not as I would have it, but trusting that you will make all things right, if I but surrender to your will. So that I may be reasonably happy in this life; and supremely happy with you forever in the next. Amen.[41]

Many soldiers were given this prayer as they left the United States for Europe; or England for Normandy on D-Day. And that's the point, surely. God hears the prayer from the trenches. God has become one of us. He has loved us enough to live for us, as one of us, and among us. He is no stranger to our despair. He is *with us* – this is what Emmanuel means. He loves us where we are, and walks with us in the valley of the shadow (Psalm 23) – he is comfort in the dark and desolate places.

'Hear my prayer, O LORD; let my cry come to you' (Psalms 102.1). He will not forsake us, even in our darkest hours. So, may almighty God give us all the faith, hope and love we need for our frail petitions.

Shepherds

Sarah Foot

> I am the good shepherd. I know my own and my own know me, just as the Father knows me and I know the Father. (John 10.14–15)

One of the publishing surprises of 2015 was the enormous success of James Rebanks's memoir *The Shepherd's Life: A Tale of the Lake District*.[42] On the face of it, Rebanks offers an unflinchingly honest account of the brutal and precarious realities of farming sheep in the unforgiving Cumbrian landscape. 'There is no beginning', he writes by way of opening, 'and there is no end. The sun rises, and falls, each day, and the seasons come and go ... We are each a tiny part of something enduring, something that feels solid, real and true.' But this is no timeless rhapsody about the satisfaction of living at one with the natural world. This is a powerful, often angry denunciation of those cultural imperialists who, ever since the eighteenth-century romantics first discovered the Lake District, have sought to create the region as a 'landscape of the imagination', a place of escape, 'where the rugged landscape and nature would stimulate feelings and sentiments that other places could not'.

A sense of continuity across generations lies at the heart of the book, which reflects as much on Rebanks's grandparents' and parents' experience of working the family farm (and on the tensions and cross-currents between and within generations) as on his own personal story. Yet at the heart of the whole narrative are the sheep. Rebanks's grandfather first farmed Swaledale ewes, tough moorland sheep, but when he bought some upland fells, he expanded into Herdwicks, the toughest mountain sheep in Britain, with a fleece so constructed that 'They are literally born dressed for a snowstorm or a rainy day.' A brief experiment that the family made in breeding one year from a French type called Charollais was never repeated: 'When the ewes had lambed it was snowing. The Herdwick lambs at two days old were racing against each other and skipping in the whiteout as if it was a sunny day. The French lambs of the same age were cowering and shivering behind the walls, and we had to lead them into the barn to keep them alive' (p. 243).

To those of us who live in the gentler landscapes of lowland Britain, and especially its urban environments, sheep play little part in our daily lives (beyond the choices we make at butchers' counters about what we want to eat). We can admire fields of sheep from the windows of our cars as we speed past, we might even take children or grandchildren to a petting zoo that has lambs. But sheep do not occupy the central place in our culture that they did in ancient Israel. They are neither so ubiquitous in the rural landscape and in each separate household as they were in first-century Palestine, nor do they have the same critical value in our modern industrialized economy, in which all agriculture makes up less than 1 per cent of GDP (0.7 per cent), and only 1.4 per cent of the British labour force now works in the agricultural sector. While the imagery of sheep and shepherding that dominates Psalm 80.1–8 and John 10.1–19 still resonates with us, we do not necessarily identify so readily as a first-century gathering will have done with the sheep, who hear and know their shepherd's voice, who turn to him not just for protection but for succour.

Yet the language of contemporary Christianity is still couched in many of the same pastoral metaphors that dominate the Scriptures. As congregations of worshippers in churches or cathedrals, we are used to being termed a 'flock'. We immediately recognize the power of the sentiments of that passage from Isaiah set as a famous chorus from Handel's *Messiah*: 'All we like sheep have gone astray; we have all turned to our own way' (Isaiah 53.6). From here it is not hard for us to see our clergy as shepherds, or pastors. The word 'pastor' that we now use both literally and figuratively to describe one who has charge of a flock, particularly one with responsibility for caring for a body of Christians, comes ultimately from the Latin verb *pāscere* to feed, or give pasture. Priests and bishops are our shepherds because they provide us, their flocks, with protective care, guidance and direction, and most importantly because they provide us with spiritual food. Imitating Christ, the good shepherd, priests aim to participate fully in the lives of their flocks, guiding, feeding and protecting them.

John 10.1–19 compresses a number of ideas in a short span, all revolving around the key verse of the whole passage: 'I am the good shepherd. The good shepherd lays down his life for the sheep' (10.11). We may divide this passage into three discrete sections. In the first, Jesus speaks directly to the Pharisees, whom he had accused of spiritual blindness at the end of the previous chapter, and who are now those who 'did not understand what he was saying to them', because they failed to listen to his words. Here we find a parable about the sheepfold. Jesus contrasts the rightful shepherd with the thief or bandit, who does not enter by the gate but climbs in another way. The sheep, who recognize their shepherd's voice, will follow him out into the pasture to feed; the stranger's voice they do not know, so they run from him.

There is a moving passage in *The Shepherd's Life* where James Rebanks describes just such an occasion when his sheep, who know him, follow him. In the depths of winter, he goes out in a snowstorm to bring his sheep off the high ground to somewhere safe from drifts where he can feed them. With his dog, Floss, he finds some of the ewes, sheltering against a wall, and the others gradually gather round, having heard his voice, pleased to eat the hay he's carried up to them. But he needs to get them off the fell. The oldest ewe follows him in the trodden path he has made, and the others come after, Indian file, while Floss brings up the rear. Rebanks reaches a gateway beyond which the ewes will be safer, but where the snow is so deep it is already higher than his waist. Unable to leave them in the lane, he pushes through the snow to make a little gully and the old ewe follows faithfully behind, bringing the rest with her. 'And then I am through the drift', he writes, 'the ground reaching back up towards my feet. I tumble over as I hit a stone, and the old ewe walks over my legs, followed by eighty others, all of which are now on a mission. They trek away down the field to where the snow is less deep, and where I can go and feed them with hay' (pp. 187–8). Here we see vividly drawn in a contemporary context what it meant for Jesus to say the shepherd of the sheep calls his own sheep by name and leads them out.

Once John in chapter 10 had defined the pastoral landscape on which the rest of what he had to say would be set, the evangelist moved on in the second section of this passage to make Jesus himself the gate of the sheepfold. Jesus is the door through whom the sheep gain access to good pasture, and the means by which the flock is protected. 'Jesus the door' offers both sustaining nourishment of the pasture and salvation; he provides abundant life. The christological focus of the middle verses becomes explicit in the third and final portion of the passage, where the image of the good shepherd links Jesus with the messianic shepherd of the people of God.

In contrasting himself with the hired hand, Jesus deploys imagery familiar from numerous passages in the Old Testament where those who failed to care adequately for God's flock, the people of Israel, left them prey to wolves. The good shepherd lays down his life for the sheep; the hired hand, on seeing the wolf coming, leaves his flock and runs away, so that the sheep are scattered (John 10.11–13). Then Jesus says again, 'I am the good shepherd' (10.14) and from this point onwards the discourse has shifted. He is no longer talking about the relationship between good and bad shepherds, or genuine shepherds and hired hands. From here on he speaks just about the relationship he has with his flock ('I know my own and my own know me', 10.14) and his relationship with the Father, with whom he is one. Playing on the idea of knowing, he stresses the mutual intimacy of his relationship with the Father: as the Father knows Jesus, so also does Jesus know the Father. Their shared knowledge and intimate understanding, the oneness between Jesus and the sheep and Jesus and the Father, leads logically to the good shepherd's laying down of his life for his sheep. Jesus is no longer the Davidic type of shepherd messiah, who gathers Israel together into one fold, but a messiah who lays down his life for his sheep because of his oneness with the Father. And so the world outside Israel is also to be brought into his sheepfold, through Jesus' willing gift of himself up to death.

But just two Sundays after the joys of Easter Day, we are brought back again to the agony of the cross. Jesus says twice, 'I am the good shepherd … who lays down [his] life for the sheep' (10.11, and also in verse 14), and we cannot but hear those verses as making direct reference to the crucifixion. But what we now know is that that act of offering himself unto death, both freely given and performed in total obedience to the Father, is not the end of the story. That is what Easter is all about. 'No one takes [my life] from me, but I lay it down of my own accord. I have power to lay it down, and I have power to take it up again' (10.18). The resurrection is not simply God's reward for his Son's obedience ('obedient to the point of death ... even death on a cross', Philippians 2.8), nor is it his rescue of a Son who was not recognized, but was made a victim by his own people. The power of the resurrection comes from Jesus' free self-giving, a giving that opens the way to life. The message for us, Christ's disciples, is clear. If freedom does not come from our arbitrary self-choosing, but is rooted in the divine will, then we need to open ourselves up to listening to his word that expresses that will; to follow his voice and to abide in the truth that ultimately will make us free (John 8.31–33).

This passage in John's Gospel is not asking us to be good shepherds. It is telling us what it means to be sheep in God's flock. Not good sheep, or bad sheep – there's no judgement here, no separation between the sheep on grounds of virtue, or between sheep and goats. Jesus does warn us to avoid the thieves and bandits of our own day (perhaps most readily translated in modern imagery to the evil of those who lure us towards the shadier sides of social media, or to excessive consumption; those who encourage, even celebrate, carelessness with the resources of our fragile world). He urges us to focus instead on him, Christ the good shepherd, who is the gate of the sheepfold. If we will only abandon our determination to be independent and self-sufficient, and just hear his call, the voice that – when we pause to listen to it properly – is so familiar, then we will hear his invitation to enter the fold, where we may find salvation, nurture and abundant life. Few of us have the capacity to make the imaginative leap that would be required to put ourselves in James Rebanks's position and lie in the snow as the gateway to a field where sheep may safely graze. But that is not what Jesus is asking us to do. All he asks of us is that we hear him when he calls us by name and, having heard him, allow him to feed us in a green pasture, and lead us out beside waters of comfort (Psalms 23.2). The author of the letter to the Hebrews states this unambiguously:

Now may the God of peace, who brought back from the dead our Lord Jesus, the great shepherd of the sheep, by the blood of the eternal covenant, make you complete in everything good so that you may do his will, working among us that which is pleasing in his sight, through Jesus Christ, to whom be the glory for ever and ever. Amen (Hebrews 13.20–21).

Odds and ends

Martyn Percy

When we think about it, there is quite a bit of gambling going on in the Bible. Pilate offers the crowd baying for blood a 50–50 choice – do you want Jesus or Barabbas? Even though it is 50–50, the odds, we sense, are already firmly stacked against Jesus. Before he is crucified, Jesus is blindfolded and invited to guess who struck him. It is a kind of cruel wager, in which the odds continue to be heavily stacked against the victim. At the end of the Gospels, the soldiers draw lots for Jesus' clothes. So at the foot of the cross, the executioners and guards play dice before God.

But there are other odds too. What are the odds of a small Jewish sect becoming the world's largest faith? No one placed a bet at the bookies on that one in AD 33. What were the odds that a key member of the disciples' team, and the treasurer no less, would lose his place to an unknown man named Matthias, the disciple and apostle chosen to replace Judas, and chosen by lottery.

I like the story of Matthias, because it shows that the first Christians knew the value of being pragmatic, and could put it before principle when needed. I suppose the better thing to do with Judas' successor was to go into a lock-down conclave, and emerge only when ready. But time is short; there is a mission to get on with. They need a twelfth apostle – preferably before supper and sunset – and so they draw lots. It's a gamble, but it seems to pay off.

But there is a deeper theme at work in the manner of Matthias' selection and it is this: we are all dispensable. Which is not to say that we don't count, or have little worth. Far from it. It is, rather, to say that God's work is not *only* accomplished through us. It was done through our predecessors; and it will be continued through our successors. Matthias is, arguably, the patron saint of those who think it all depends on them. Judas is airbrushed out of history and memory, and the up-until-now-unknown runner called Matthias reminds us that God is not short on the supply-side for people he can continue to work with. God hasn't played dice with anyone, mind you. But he does know a thing or two about the odds of his purpose being worked out. And I would not bet against the outcome.

So in Isaiah 22.15–22, Eliakim and the son of Hilkiah will carry forward the next stage of God's purpose. And Paul, in Philippians 3—4, has some advice about how to carry ourselves: '[forget] what lies behind and straining forward to what lies ahead' (Philippians 3.13) – because we will meet God in his resurrection power: the power of Easter, and of new life. But, adds Paul, hold on to what you have attained already, because you may need it.

Paul's call in Philippians is for both resilience and vision. He is not asking us to gamble – merely to remember that there are no reliable odds on how the future will turn out. But the God of the present – and of the future – will not let you down. So we do not need to live as others might, because the 'citizenship of heaven', as Paul calls it, will see that we are in the end held and cherished by a God who will not let us go.

I think Matthias might have agreed with that well-known quip by Woody Allen: 'If you want to make God laugh, tell him about your plans.' But it turns out all right if you trust in God for the future. God is faithful; and the simple thing that is asked of us is to step out in faith too. Matthias had to; so did his electors. So now do we. Never mind the odds – what are the ends?

Love Actually

Graham Ward

Here I want to talk about love, love in the context of a verse from Isaiah 49: 'The LORD God hath called me from the womb; from the bowels of my mother hath he made mention of my name' (Isaiah 49.1, KJV). I cite the King James Authorized Version, for there's a balance and poetry that gives Isaiah's sentiment gravitas. And it's gravitas that I want to get at, because Isaiah relates calling to our being created, to who we are and how we are named – not by ourselves, but by God who 'hath … made mention of my name'. We are called into being before we begin to exist. Love is not just the expression of who and what we are as created in God's good providence; love is the means, the way, whereby we come to know who and what we are. In loving we know we are alive, as Ed Sheeran sings, and it can hurt sometimes.

There is a story at the end of John 21 that to my mind sums up the nature of Christian discipleship: the famous dialogue between the risen Christ and Peter. The exchange about following Jesus centres around the question 'Do you love me?' The risen Jesus asks Peter three times: 'Do you love me more than these?' Those with a knowledge of Greek will point to how the word used for 'love' changes. Christ uses, in his first two questions to Peter, the Greek verb *agapao* (a deep loving related to the way God loves us; a love that abandons itself towards what is other). Peter replies throughout with the Greek verb *phileo* (a loving that can be between two married people, but it is often associated with friendship). The third time Christ asks his question of Peter he uses the verb Peter uses – *phileo*. It's as if the new discipleship Peter has come into following the resurrection, and the knowledge he is forgiven for his betrayal of Christ on Good Friday, cannot yet understand love as *agape* or dare not describe his love as *agape* because of what he still remembers.

But whether we use *agapao* or *phileo*, the question Christ puts to Peter is the most basic question that Christ can ask of any who follow him; it's the basic ecclesiological question of belonging to Christ, of being *in* Christ. But as Peter seems to recognize by his confusion at being asked the questions, the one who asks this is the one who knows all things, God. Christ is therefore not asking Peter this question because he doesn't know the answer. He is asking it because Peter needs to know something – something about his own disposition now towards Christ; something that has changed because of the Easter events. Peter needs to know that he loves – and maybe that his loving, though beginning and ending in friendship, has to become something more self-sacrificial. It has to pour itself out. Second, Peter has to recognize that such self-abandoning loving will carry consequences. Three times he is commanded to feed or nourish Jesus' lambs; tend, guide, govern his sheep; and feed or nourish them.

To love in Christ installs us in a delicate web of relations, a web as fragile and diaphanous as the web of a spider frosted on one of Britain's bright winter mornings. These relations are vibrant with life and light and darkness and tension. But it is only in and through this web of relations that we will ever come to know Christ as the way, the truth and the life: relations to ourselves; relations to Christ; and relations to others. There are no relations to ourselves or to Christ without relations to others. In this web of relations Peter himself will be hollowed out by that loving. That's what loving does. It hollows out because it demands a giving-up – mainly of our self-preoccupation – in order to be given a true name in Christ. *But*, and this is crucial: being hollowed out *in Christ* is the most positive experience of redemption.

Paul, in his Letter to the Philippians, puts this hollowing out into a Christological context often referred to as kenosis. The word comes from the Greek verb *keneo*, which means 'to pour out', and the opposite of empty is *plereo*, 'to fill up'. Paul plays with these two words. Christ pours himself out for us in his obedience to the Father – an 'obedience even unto death', Paul tell us. But the flip side of this pouring out and giving up of self is that he is 'highly exalted' and given 'the name that is above every name, so that at the name of Jesus every knee should bend, in heaven and on earth and under the earth, and every tongue should confess that Jesus Christ is Lord, to the glory of God the Father' (Philippians 2.9–11).

Being hollowed out in Christ *is* our redemption because it enables us to participate in him, be one with him, and so enter into his exaltation. So what all of us are called to is to love as a labour of self-offering. Isaiah tells God, 'I have laboured in vain, I have spent my strength for nothing' (Isaiah 49.4). But God corrects him. The labour has not been in vain. The labour in the love of Christ is an operation of the love of Christ in the world. It is never in vain. It *will* help to bring about, in its own small way, 'salvation unto the end of the earth'. As a labour, love is a craft we have to learn, a craft in which we too have our being crafted. This love has to discipline all our desires, and this disciplining is so vital to discipleship it cannot be done in our own strength. 'I have the power to lay down my life,' Jesus tells his disciples, earlier in John's Gospel.

We don't have that power. If loving is done in our own strength then what the hollowing out, pouring out and self-giving produces can be dangerously negative and have violent emotional and physiological effects. The power of love comes from elsewhere. It comes from beyond us because it is beyond us. It comes from God; it is God in action, God as pure energy and operation. It is a divine outpouring out of which all things were created, in which we ourselves have our being. We are here because of love; love is written into our nature and our destiny. In all our loving of other people we are living out something of that divine love, that divine name that 'he hath made mention of'. We are exploring and experiencing that which is divine. In all our loving we come to participate in Christ as the way, the truth and the life.

A while back, the primates of the Anglican Communion met at Lambeth Palace in London, and the topic they were discussing was one that is tearing them apart: homosexuality. In their verdict on the American Episcopalian Church's appointment of an openly gay bishop, it was clear that homosexuals are a problem for many in the Anglican Communion. And the Church of England, with its own long and venerable tradition, is now subject to the rulings of the Anglican Communion. This is a Communion formed in, through and beyond its colonialism. What I am expressing here they would condemn. I am saying that the love of which I speak – its hurts, the times when it is hard, its rootedness in learning about

Christ, and in our being called to be who we are by God from the wombs of our mothers – is exactly that: love actually. Whether that love is between a man and a woman, between two women, or between two men. The redemptive power and self-emptying of such love cannot be denied. I am not going to argue about its rights and wrongs, because this is not a moral issue. Love between consenting adults, between two human beings, in and through all the mysteries and creative energies of attraction, desire and embodiment is not a moral issue.

But the treatment of gay people by the Church as second-class members or deviants from the gospel or disabled in some way *is* a moral problem. Persecution *is* a moral problem, just as injustice *is* a moral problem. I'm not even calling for tolerance. In the face of the hollowing out that loving involves, tolerance is a mealy mouthed word that often masks indifference. I am calling for celebration; the celebration of a God-given gift and destiny coming from nothing less than that calling 'from the bowels of my mother' and that 'mention of my name'. It is the way Christ is learnt and encountered, and 'salvation unto the end of the world' is proclaimed and wrought.

In my pastoral capacity I have heard of Anglican diocesan directors of ordinands refusing to allow gay people to go forward for ordination until they repent. I have heard of bishops refusing to find parishes for those who have realized who they are while training. I have talked to people from Jamaica and several African countries who have come to Oxford to study for a year, and speak of their terror in returning home. I have met others who have to live lies because their careers would be on the line. I have even mourned the suicide or attempted suicide of a few. And, once, I encountered the sheer overwhelming beauty of an evangelical family deeply wounded by their son's coming out to them, but who slowly came to see he was the same person they had always known – only much, much happier. And they repented, and the son and his partner were welcomed and embraced. And all of us witnessed what salvation in Christ looks like.

So, let us live, let us love, let us be who we are, how we were created. We have a testimony, carved out through pain and struggle, joy and betrayal, hope and disappointment, and the need to be honest with ourselves. We then have a faithful witness to the gospel of Jesus Christ.

Christian unity at Jacob's Well

Martyn Percy

According to one Hollywood film, a Methodist is basically a Baptist who has been taught to read. This definition, you might like to know, is attributed to a Presbyterian minister. But as any Methodist will tell you, a Presbyterian is someone for whom Methodism is a bit too racy. This is not unlike the definition of an actuary – someone who finds accountancy just too exciting. (Presbyterian, by the way, is an anagram of Britney Spears – although it is not immediately clear how this might benefit either party.)

These waspish caricatures, amusing though they might be, are symptomatic of a bygone era of inter-denominational wars. For most of the population, religious identity is centred not on the faith of their parents, but on just what happens to be good and local. Ecclesial brand loyalty is a dying phenomenon.

It was not always so. Once upon a time, denominational names mattered a great deal, although their origin is often forgotten. It remains the case that very few denominations chose their own name. 'Anglicanism' is a term that was popularized by James VI of Scotland, and contains a degree of mocking irony. Similarly, 'Anabaptists' had their family name bestowed upon them by their detractors. Equally, 'Methodist' can also be read as a dubious compliment – another mildly derogatory 'nickname'.

And yet any uninitiated observer might be forgiven for thinking that not much has changed. The ecumenical movement has not yet sighted the promised land of Unity. Indeed, if anything, many churches seem to be specializing in fragmentation and exacerbating their differences. Arguments over gender, sexuality and other issues seem to mock the prayer of Jesus, 'that they may all be one'.

And so to the story of an encounter between Jesus and an un-named woman at Jacob's Well. But first some history. The well is still in Israel, in Nablus, on the West Bank. Built over

it is a Greek monastery, and it was here, in 1979, that Soph-
ocles Hasapis, the parish priest and guardian of the well, lost
his life. He was killed by fundamentalist Jewish settlers, who
resented the presence of the small community of monks there,
and the Christian shrine built on and over what they felt was
a sacred Jewish site. They gouged out his eyes, and cut off his
hands while he was saying vespers. Then they threw a grenade
into the church.

Religion, as we know, is an affair of the heart as much as of
the head. It inspires great passion – love and, of course, hate.
Every act of terrorism serves to remind us what people will do in
the name of their God. The history of Christian behaviour is, of
course, no better than other faiths.

To some extent, the encounter that Jesus has at Jacob's Well
with the un-named woman is all about those same dynamics. Contested space and arguments over what is sacred and what might
be secular; hatred and fear of people who see faith differently. It's
all there. Religious extremism is more like a cry of despair than a
shout of hope, which partly accounts for the narrow and negative
nature of belief that sectarianism normally breeds. However, it
would be a mistake to assume that purity and power are only
issues for small and kraal-like religious groups. Purity and power
are issues for all Christians and all churches and fundamentalism
and extremism as a phenomenon is simply a concentration of a
'problem' that affects many different faiths, including all forms of
Christianity – including those that espouse liberalism or openness.
Boundaries of definition can quickly become borders marking
territory and, ultimately, barriers.

And it is into this that Jesus walks. As he is returning to Galilee,
we are treated to a story about water and wells that never run dry.
But before he can get to Galilee from Judea, he must pass through
Samaria – he has to cross a region that is, by definition, a place
of taint and compromise that is normally to be avoided. But Jesus
does not *need* to pass through Samaria; he could have chosen
the route that follows the Jordan Valley, and avoids Samaria. So
John's Gospel, in stating that Jesus 'had' to pass through Samaria,
is not making a cartographical point; Jesus chooses this route in
the same way that the son of man 'must' suffer (Mark 8.31) –

the accent is on Jesus' obligation to a deeper path that remains concealed from most of those who follow him. This is why Jesus arrives at the town of Sychar (John 4.5–6), where he then sits at Jacob's Well (thereby linking Jesus with the patriarchs), with John telling us that Jesus is 'tired'. It is the sixth hour, the middle of the day.

And it is here that the Samaritan woman enters the story. The time of day for entry is critical, as it suggests her marginality. Water is traditionally drawn at dusk or early in the morning. But the sixth hour is noon, when the sun is at its hottest, suggesting that this woman's company is questionable; she is something of an outsider even within her own community.

Because in John's Gospel the woman is unnamed, this can be interpreted as a code for 'undesirable', or even 'sinner' – the latter term having more of a social than ethical significance in the first century. What is startling, therefore, is Jesus' direct address to her: 'give me a drink'. Furthermore, notes John, the disciples have all left to buy provisions: there is no mutual hospitality between Jews and Samaritans. This means that Jesus and the woman are alone.

On one level, this request can be read as a gesture of reconciliation. Jesus asks something of a Samaritan, and a woman. Jesus needs her help, and he asks for it. But this gesture is, of course, met with astonishment: 'how can you ask anything of me, a Samaritan?' And the response from Jesus only serves to widen her eyes, for Jesus states that if she knew who she was talking to and what God gives, it is she who would be asking for water – 'living water'. Or, more accurately, in the Greek this is 'running water' – the kind that echoes that which *flows* from the rock in the desert from the staff of Moses.

John is, in other words, making a contrast between the still, perhaps even stale, water of the well, and the water of life that Jesus speaks of. This is a water that, literally, brings life. The conversation, like the depth of the well, goes another stage deeper at this point. The woman's question becomes laced with rhetorical tropes: are you greater than Jacob? Where do you get this living water from? John turns the woman's astonishment into curiosity – she wades into the deeper waters of the conversation. And

again, the conversation turns on what seems like a staged arti-
ficiality in order to draw the woman in even deeper. Jesus says:
'Everyone who drinks of this water will be thirsty again, those
who drink of the water that I will give them will never be thirsty'
(John 4.13–14).

The Well, just as it was violently contested in 1979, was also
contested in Jesus' day. Here we have a sacred site in disputed
ownership. But Jesus' ministry returns the Well to common
ownership. By reaching out to the woman, and talking about the
true water of life, he is asking us to put our differences aside, and
focus on the deep unity we share. Ultimately, unity cannot be
imposed: it has to be discovered and cultivated organically.

So what lessons can we learn for unity from Jacob's Well, Jesus
and the Samaritan woman? The story ends as it began – with a
tale of an unexpected encounter, with themes of taint, surprise
and boundary crossing redolent in the text. A group of Samaritans now come to see Jesus, prompted by the un-named woman.
This in turn prompts an excursus from Jesus about the harvest
– a cipher for God's abundance, but also judgement. It is now
obvious, though (if also perhaps puzzling to the disciples), that
Jesus, throughout this encounter, is making a profound series
of political statements about the nature of the kingdom and the
Messiah. We can summarize these briefly.

First, it is God who, in Christ, comes to the Samaritans, and
engages with them on their own territory and in their own idiom
and dialect. We have to remember that this was not the obvious
route for Jesus to take to get to Galilee – he chose to deviate, and
allowed himself to be distracted.

Second, the message to the Samaritans is not 'become a Jew like
me', but rather 'there is a time when tribal boundaries will cease
to matter', and genuine faith will not be about which party, sect
or denomination one belongs to, but instead be about 'spirit and
truth'.

Third, this is a story of radical inclusiveness. As is so often the
case in the Gospels, Jesus is fraternizing with people who raise
questions of taste, discernment and even purity. But Jesus is not
interested in the labels we give one another. This is all about
grace. Jesus meets us all on the level.

Jesus' work with the Samaritans carries an important message for unity. For Jesus, in reaching out to the Samaritans as equals, makes a decisive contribution to that elusive search for true unity – one that respects the dignity of difference. And in the midst of that, what may also be discovered is that difference is not a sign of weakness, but rather of strength. The diversity within the wider Church has always been one of its most glorious treasures. It has created the possibility of staying within a faith yet changing, and of moving to and from traditions, yet without abandoning the denomination. Christians need pray only one prayer for unity week: 'may we all be one – but thank God we are all different'.

Debating the trivial things: tactics and strategies

Martyn Percy

Some years ago David Beckham, it is said, was invited to speak to a hushed, awe-struck school assembly in a suburb of Manchester. The headmaster duly introduced the world-famous football player in laudatory tones. Mr Beckham then duly stepped up to the podium, and spoke these words, 'They are small, rounded and very minty – there are other flavours too, but spearmint is best – and they come in packs of forty in a small plastic dispenser. I warmly recommend them.' Then he sat down. There was a rather awkward silence, and then the headmaster leaned over and whispered, 'Mr Beckham, we asked you to talk about *tactics*.' (So not Tic-Tacs, if you haven't already got the joke!)

I don't know about you, but I really love the last chapters of the Book of Acts. They are pretty Machiavellian, really. It is Paul at his best, out-witting, out-foxing and out-narrating his critics and persecutors. And it's the tactics that I love. Paul, even with his back to the wall, and with no way out, seems to be a kind of holy Houdini. Just when there is no escape, he somehow wriggles free. And were this just an adventure story – a kind of 'Religious Ripping Yarn' – we probably would not read Acts at all today. But the Book of Acts functions as a pivot and rivet in the New

Testament, linking the breathless, compelling stories of the Gospels with the pastoral and ecclesial wisdom of the Epistles.

Scholars from business and management schools have been known to try to draw a careful distinction between strategy and tactics. Strategies, they say, are the foundational core beliefs and vision. Tactics are all about implementation, to reach the goal of the strategy or objective. So the strategy or the objective might be to win the war, yet as German military strategist Helmuth von Moltke sagely noted, 'no battle plan survives contact with the enemy'. So you may have an objective, but you must be prepared to change tactics and game plans several times if you want to achieve your strategy. When your plan meets the real world, the real world wins. Nothing goes as planned. Errors pile up. Mistaken suppositions come back to bite you. The most brilliant plan loses touch with reality.

But – and it is a big 'but' here – the Church has an objective and strategy that is not up for negotiation. It is summarized in the law and it is reflected in Deuteronomy 10.12–13. In modern idiom, we might say, the summary of the law that Jesus gives us in the Gospels is what God will not change. Not ever. Love the Lord your God with all your heart, mind, soul and strength. Love your neighbour as yourself. Everything hangs on these statements. They are not up for negotiation.

Urban T. Holmes closes his book *What is Anglicanism?* with these words:

> All religious questions merge into the one query: What shall we do? There is an inevitable course to our religious profession, which can be aborted only by denying its Lord. That course leads to living in the world as God sees the world. We can debate the trivial points, but the vision is largely clear. To love God is to relieve the burden of all who suffer. The rest is a question of tactics ...[43]

Holmes adds that it is possible for a Christian to refuse to see the implications of Christ for his or her manner of living. It is a blasphemy to suggest that this is a matter of indifference to God. It is not. There is nothing outside God's business. God speaks, and we as Christians must discern what he says to us now, in this place.

That's why I am sometimes tempted to remark that we can summarize the Old Testament in one word, if we really want to. The word is 'wait'. Wait for God. Wait for God's timing. Wait in exile. Wait in exodus. Do not try and get out of Babylon too fast, because God is using this time – this waiting time – to teach and chastise. So, wait. Wait for deliverance; and wait for the Messiah. Good things come to those who wait. But the word that summarizes the New Testament is simply 'go'. Go and do likewise. Go and do what Christ has done. Go out into all the world. Go and feed the poor, visit the prisoner; go and baptize. The early Church is not about bums on pews. It is about bums off pews, and into the streets and cities. Go.

The Church, of course, does not find it easy to live like this. We don't like waiting very much. And we'd like to stay right where we are, and for others to go. We get easily distracted by peripheral issues in the Church, such as sexuality or gender.

The journalist and broadcaster Jeremy Paxman once quipped that the Church of England believes that there is no issue that cannot be eventually solved over a cup of tea in the vicar's study. This waspish compliment directed towards Anglicanism serves to remind us that many regard its polity as being quintessentially peaceable and polite, in which matters never really get too out of hand.

In theological disputes, such as those over the ordination of women, part of the strategy that enables unity can be centred on containing some of the more passionate voices in the debate. Extreme feelings, when voiced, can lead to extreme reactions. And extreme reactions, when allowed full vent, can make situations unstable. Nations fall apart; communions fracture; families divide. Things said briefly in the heat of a moment can cause wounds that may take years to heal. Often, congregational unity in the midst of disputes can only be secured by finding an open, middle way, in which the voices of moderation and tolerance occupy the central ground, enabling the Church to move forwards.

For leaders, this means of course continually listening to the experiences that lead to anger, and trying to see them from the perspective of those with less power. It means humility on the part of those who hold power, and an acknowledgement of the fear of losing power and control. It means a new way of looking at power relationships that takes the gospel seriously in their equal-izing and levelling. This is one of the most demanding aspects of oversight: namely, having the emotional intelligence, patience and empathy to hold feelings, anger, disappointment and frustration – other people's as well as your own. Episcopacy, it seems to me, is less about strategy and more about deeply learnt poise, especially in holding together competing convictions and trying to resolve deep conflicts.

But before conflicts can be resolved, they must first of all be *held*. And here we find another of the most demanding aspects of oversight within the context of considerable theological and cul-tural diversity. Because one of the tasks of the Church is to soak up sharp and contested issues, in such a way as to limit and blunt the possibility of deep intra- and inter-personal damage being caused, as well as further dislocation in people's sense of faith-ful identity. Retaining composure, and somehow holding people together who would otherwise divide (due to the nature of their intense and competing convictions), is a stretching vocation. Any-one exercising a ministry of oversight will understand the costly nature of this vocation.

Much of Anglican polity is 'open' in its texture; and although it has a shape, it is none the less unresolved and incomplete. There-fore, issues that cannot be determined often require being 'held'; a deliberate postponement of resolution. Put another way, there is a tension between being an identifiable community with creeds and fundaments; and yet also being a body that recognizes that some issues are essentially un-decidable in the Church. Indeed, 'Anglican un-decidability' (a phrase coined by the writer Stephen Pickard) may turn out to be one of the chief counter-cultural Anglican virtues; it is very far from being a 'leadership problem', as some appear to believe.

The desire and need to sometimes reach provisional settlements that do not achieve closure is itself part of the deep 'habit of wis-dom' that has helped to form Anglican polity down the centuries. There is, of course, a typical Anglican leadership habit, embody-ing a necessary humility and holiness in relation to matters of truth, but without losing sight of the fact that difficult decisions still need to be made.

All of which leads us to the final chapters of Acts. What is perhaps striking is the lengths to which the priests and elders will go to silence Paul – an ambush and an assassination are planned (23.12–35). Paul, tactically, sidesteps this. But we should not lose sight of the vehemence and prejudice at work in this story. It is reminiscent of a key passage in *Alice's Adventures in Wonderland*:

> 'Let the jury consider their verdict,' the King said, for about the twentieth time that day. 'No, no!' said the Queen. 'Sentence first – verdict afterwards.' 'Stuff and nonsense!' said Alice loudly. 'The idea of having the sentence first!' 'Hold your tongue!' said the Queen, turning purple. 'I won't!' said Alice. 'Off with her head!' the Queen shouted at the top of her voice. Nobody moved. 'Who cares for you?' said Alice (she had grown to her full size by this time). 'You're nothing but a pack of cards!'

'You're nothing but a pack of cards' is, essentially, half of what Paul is saying to his critics. Paul's critics made their minds up before he had finished speaking; they passed sentence before they reached a verdict. We sometimes say such things too easily in our churches. We forget that more unites us than divides us. To return to Urban Holmes's closing words in *What is Anglicanism?* He writes: '[Our] course leads to living in the world as God sees the world. We can debate the trivial points, but the vision is largely clear. To love God is to relieve the burden of all who suffer. The rest is a question of tactics.'

Can it really come down to tactics? Yet that is all Paul is doing in Acts 23.12–35 – tactics. Because the essentials are given: love the Lord your God with all your heart, mind, soul and strength. And love your neighbour as yourself. After that, everything else is, indeed, tactics.

Story

The Free-market Church[44]

MARTYN PERCY

Written and published in the early 1990s, and at the height of
free-market ideology triumphing in Britain, this story asks what
might happen if the Church were to adopt the same economic,
political and ideological pulses that were also shaping the nation?
There are quirky details here that seem quaint now: the invention
of the portable fax machine has not come to pass in quite the way
one might have envisaged decades ago. Technology has developed
even faster with mobile phones, tablets and handheld computers.
But that is not the point. As church polity is increasingly shaped
by market forces, and by targets, strategies and plans – representing a kind of rather inward-looking cluster of concerns that are
clothed in apparently missional rhetoric – the story might serve as
a timely, even prophetic, caution.

The Church may sometimes seem down, but it is never out. Just
when secularization or consumerism seem to have triumphed,
spring, buds and new life appear. Winter passes, as it must. Yet
one problem the Church always faces never changes: namely,
coping with the overwhelming abundance of God. Knowing this
is how we come to understand that re-charting the Church is not
only a possibility: it is an inevitability. The re-enchantment of
the Church will be one where we turn aside from tribalism, and
rediscover our breadth; where we learn to value again the deep,
mellow, passionate, wise, pastoral corporeal polity we know
as Anglicanism. A Church rooted in the love of God, the ever-
generous providence of the Father, the generative power of the
Spirit, and the limitless grace of Jesus Christ; a place where there
is no coda or finale – only beginnings and openings.

Preface to the story: the real present

'We're in the last chance saloon,' said Pete Broadbent, Bishop of Willesden and one of the architects of Reform and Renewal. 'All the demographic evidence shows that, unless we do something in the next five or ten years, we're shot. There are those who say this [programme] is alien and who want to dig their heels in, but we're facing a demographic time bomb.'

The evidence was 'indisputable', said John Spence, chair of the Church's finance committee and a former Lloyds Bank executive. 'Twenty years ago the demographics matched the population as a whole. Now we're 20 years older than the population. Unless we do something, the Church will face a real crisis.' Among the changes is a redistribution of funding, largely away from struggling rural parishes to churches in deprived urban areas and those seen as innovative and energetic in adapting to social change:

> 'Some dioceses are being funded to do not very much,' said Broadbent. 'And some dioceses are underfunded, but are doing an amazing job in trying circumstances. It's about how we divvy up the money to go to places that can use it well and have the greatest need.'[45]

The story of *The Churchgoer's Charter*

The time is set some years in the future. The story is in five parts.

Present-future

The bright flash and camera lights of the nation's press reporters filled the Hall at Church House. The Bishop of Southbury, Michael Talent, blinked. Flanked by bishops, plus other officials from Church House and Sir Marcus Lloyd from the Church Commissioners, Bishop Michael began his speech:

> Ladies and Gentlemen. As you will know, today sees the launch of one of the most important documents the Church of England has produced this century ... even though we are less than a few decades into a new millennium. The House of Bishops has felt for some time that the Church is too unwieldy in its

structure to meet the needs of the people. There has been too much bureaucracy and red tape, and not enough action. Congregations have declined in number: confidence in the Church has dwindled. Today we hope to put the Church of England back on the road to recovery, with the launch of *The Churchgoer's Charter*. This will give power back to the people, and will make clergy and churches more accountable to the parishes they are supposed to be serving ...

Bishop Michael held up the glossy volume; camera motors whirred, and journalists began punching copy into their portable faxes. 'This will look great in the papers,' thought the Bishop to himself. He was right. The headlines and leader columns were fulsome in their praise. *The Times* wrote a lead article under the caption 'Bishop Sees Red [Tape]'; 'Bishop Prunes Vine', reported *The Telegraph*; 'Weeding the Weedy Church', trumpeted *The Sun*, lauding the Bishop in an article on page seven.

The Churchgoer's Charter had all begun after the government had been re-elected in 2015. It was the Prime Minister's idea. Britain's drift towards becoming a Republic had been sealed with the suspension of the House of Lords, now replaced by a new Upper House of Senators. Key posts, such as 'Archbishop of Canterbury', had become Cabinet positions, the Archbishop now being the 'Minister for Church Affairs'. It was inevitable, really, that the government and Church now worked together more closely. Cathedrals had been identified as major tourist attractions and potential income earners as long as 30 years ago.

When the government had stepped in to help rebuild and refurbish some cathedrals, and then the Church Commissioners had applied for Euro-loan, it had opened the way for church and state to co-operate at levels unknown since the days of the Reformation. One day, over coffee, the Prime Minister had chatted informally to the Archbishop about 'opening up the Church to the ordinary people ... making ministers more accountable to their parishes ... streamlining services, and capitalizing on investments and ministries'. The fruit of their dialogue was a Republican commission, chaired by the Bishop of Southbury. And now, today, here was *The Churchgoer's Charter*.

Two years later

For the Revd Maurice Green, *The Churchgoer's Charter* had been a godsend. His flourishing eclectic church in a prosperous university town had been one of the first to opt out of the diocese of Southbury. As a self-governing body, they were now free from many of the diocesan central structures that they felt had held them back from competing effectively with other churches. They had stopped paying their quota. They had always found it uncomfortable supporting a broad Church; all those causes, churches and theological outlooks they had never liked could now fend for themselves. Besides this, they had 'rationalized' their giving to charities and outside bodies, in favour of concentrating their resources on the local situation.

The results had been spectacular. Three fizzy new curates had been hired: the duff old one the diocese provided had been made redundant. The new administrator, together with a new full-time accountant, had identified the areas of ministry that were most profitable. Fees for baptisms, weddings and funerals were set at market rates. A new building programme provided further opportunities for income-bearing outreach. The Church Flower Shop provided all tributes, displays and bouquets for weddings and funerals. The new Church Brasserie (the Cana Wine Bar) did the catering for all special events; it was already featured in the *Les Routiers Guide*. A local photographer was awarded the exclusive contract for all weddings at the church, after it had been put out to competitive tender. Certain hymns and prayers had attracted sponsorship from local companies. A local building firm was always mentioned when 'The Church is One Foundation' was sung; the local privatized electricity board sponsored the Collect for Evening Prayer, 'Lighten Our Darkness'.

Alas, other parishes had not been nearly so innovative. Some had obviously just not used their talents as wisely. Of the fourteen churches in the town, six had already shut in two years, or been forced to merge. Of course, where possible, the stronger churches had attempted to cover areas that were now no longer served by a parish priest. But in some of the poorer estates on the fringe of town this had proved problematic. Providing a spiritual service at a realistic cost was difficult, especially when some of the people living in impoverished urban areas seemed 'to want something for nothing'. The Revd Maurice Green did feel some sadness about this, yet he comforted himself with the proverb that 'Sheep always go where the grass is'. People would come to church if it offered a good service: it wasn't his fault if some clergy buried their talents.

Three years later

Bishop Michael of Southbury sat in his study. The rain poured down outside. 'Ah, where on earth has it all gone wrong?' he sighed. He had some answers, of course, but they were painful to face. For example, there was the share issue in the Church of England, launched in 2020. Called *20–20 Vision: Your Share In the Future*, congregations had been encouraged to buy shares in the national Church, which entitled them to discounts for weddings, funerals and baptisms, and a small dividend each year if the Church Commissioners' property speculation had gone well. It had been difficult to get off the ground initially, but the message had soon got home. The Share Issue would allow the public a greater say in how the Church was run, and in its future direction.

To Bishop Michael, it had seemed the natural follow-up to *The Churchgoer's Charter*, which had already brought sweeping changes. Administrative posts had been cut by a half in his diocese. Education, Welfare and Social Responsibility officers had been pushed into 'private practice', so churches that needed them could purchase their services when they required them. The poorer parishes that had relied on them far too much in the past were now being encouraged to discover their own resources. Parishes had merged, inefficient clergy laid off, and non-cost-effective areas of ministry identified and re-prioritized. As far as the Bishop was concerned, this was all excellent. However, it had got out of control. The agenda of *The Churchgoer's Charter* seemed like an unstoppable train. Now it looked as though he, the Bishop (of all people), was in danger of losing his job.

The problem had begun six months before when the more cost-effective parishes in his diocese had got together with other like-minded churches from neighbouring dioceses. They had taken a comprehensive look at synodical and ecclesiastical structures. A clergyman from his own diocese, the Revd Maurice Green, had argued that bishops were too many and too expensive: 'they confirm some people in your church once a year, ordain you a new curate every four years and for that they get a hundred grand, a jolly nice house and a chauffeur-driven car! They're simply not worth it.'

Changes soon followed. Quotas were again withheld by wealthy parishes until all bishops signed up for the 'ERM' – the Episcopal Exchange Rate Mechanism. The idea was to let bishops 'float', and open up competition. They would no longer get the exclusive contract for a diocese. Those who did good confirmation addresses or retreats would be paid for their services; those who didn't would be gradually laid off. Some bishops had already gone into 'private practice', specializing in confirmations, ordinations, dedications, after-dinner speeches or radio broadcasts. However, for the Bishop of Southbury, the writing was on the wall: he knew he couldn't compete with some of the younger, more dynamic bishops. His letter of resignation was prepared, and sat on the table. He was going to go on a very long retreat.

Four years later

Sitting in the Hall at Church House, Michael Talent, now the former Bishop of Southbury, must have thought he'd seen it all before. Masses of cameramen, journalists, photographers and soundmen lined up six or seven deep waiting for him to speak. He was not flanked by other bishops this time. The only endorsement he had was a letter from his friend, the former Archbishop of Canterbury, who'd retired early due to ill health.

He began to speak, this time holding aloft a copy of a new book written by him, called *Faith in Society.* Its message, he said, was simple. You cannot place a value on spiritual service. Everyone is entitled to ministry, whether they can afford it or not. The National Church Service must be there for all its people, not just a few. The richer churches must support the poorer ones, even if it cost them so much that it hurt them. An apparently weak and 'broad' Church is probably better placed to serve society than a handful of strong eclectic ones. True, the Church is accountable to people, but also to God, the maker and judge of us all.

One journalist asked him where all this fresh vision had come from. In reply, Michael Talent said it was actually quite an old vision, but it hadn't been given a fair hearing. He referred to the Parable of the Talents, pointing out that most people thought that this was about wise financial investment. 'But,' he added, 'It is really about people and truth as well: they need to be invested in too, not buried out of fear. And sometimes apparently attractive gains need to be sacrificed; after all, we are called to lose our lives, not win them.' As he was speaking and replying to questions, journalists shuffled, looked irritated, and then began to leave.

'I bet this won't look very good in the newspapers tomorrow,' he thought. And he was right. They didn't print a word of it.

Postscript – ten years later

Retirement rather agreed with Bishop Michael. It had given him the chance to reflect on the changes that had come about in recent years, especially as a number of them had been something of a surprise. For example, he could not have predicted the fate of the Revd Maurice Green. His church had witnessed enormous growth in the early years of new development. But the constant demands to make the buildings and projects financially viable had led to compromises, and also to divisive and fractious church meetings. The Victorian gallery in the church – a huge space – had been converted into a fitness centre, complete with a glass wall that allowed those attending the gym to watch services as they lifted weights, ran on the machines, and exercised on the benches.

It had seemed like a good idea at the time. Come to church and get fit; pay a subscription too, and witness some worship. And why not stay for a Fairtrade drink in the café after? ('Sweat, Sacrament, Divine', ran the advertisement.) But some of the worshippers – even dyed-in-the-wool modernizers – had objected. They did not think that their church was a place for a gym. Some objected that worship was now confused: could people really give their all to God if at the same time they were also thinking about their weight, their fitness, and how they looked? The outsourcing of the Cana Wine Bar and café to a new catering company who paid good money for the franchise, but sat light to the ethos of the Church, had also caused complications.

The church was still making money, and still had many members, but something was missing. Some worshippers felt the soul had gone from the place. Then the economic recession, which hit everyone and everything in its path, bit swiftly and deeply. Suddenly, church meetings were consumed by talks of mergers, redundancies, outsourcing and rationalizations. Added to which, some worshippers just started to drift off to a local church with far fewer members, and no apparent entrepreneurial outlook at all – but one that apparently had something that Maurice's church didn't: a soul. And a sense of awe and wonder, with a priest you could see in the week without going through a plethora of PAs and administrators. The church members were restless for change.

When Maurice's post came up for renewal, everything was basically fine: the recession was weathered; the income streams back on track; the number of worshippers steadied, having stemmed the earlier haemorrhaging. But the Church Council did not renew Maurice's contract. They thanked him for all he had done, but said that they felt God wanted to do something new with the church. To return it to being a place of sacredness and peace; a house of prayer; and an oasis of stillness. People wanted a change of direction; not what Maurice offered.

He left with a handsome pay-off – but somewhat bitter, and also curious. He remembered – from years ago at seminary – another pastor's words. Was it Niemoller, from Germany? He wasn't sure. But the gist of it was this.

First the market forces came for the weaker parishes; but I didn't say anything. Then they came for the clergy who were deemed not to be successful or useful; but I didn't say anything. Then they came for the officers and administrators supporting the weaker parishes and clergy; and I didn't say anything. Then they came for the people who had introduced the change-management – for they too were expendable – and I didn't say anything. Then finally they came for me. But there was no one left to speak for me.

Maurice Green's church had hired a new pastor – a former

monk, called Benedict – who had not much in the way of business acumen, and little in the way of charismatic or dynamic leadership. There was not much money about any more, and little in the way of numerical or financial growth. But Benedict prayed for his people, visited faithfully, and was seen about in the parish. The Cana Wine Bar was taken back into ownership by the church, and the space used to feed the poor. The gym and fitness centre went out of business, and now housed bunk-beds for the homeless.

Had the entrepreneurial church failed? It was hard to say. But the congregation seemed happy enough. There was energy for mission, but no longer the ersatz of chimera-consumerist Christianity. Something earthy and authentic was now coming into existence. Benedict talked about the church in a different way. His church, he said, was a safe space to trespass; a place for finding divine peace; a symbol of diversity in unity; and a Pentecostal laboratory. He said it was a theatre of basic drama and a centre for creativity. It was a temple of dialogue and an academy of committed information; and a place for international exchange. He called the church to be a clinic for public exorcism; a broadcasting station for the voice of the poor; and a tower of reconciliation. He suggested that the ministry of the church was to be a motel for pilgrims – and a house of vicarious feasts. It was to be a hut for the shepherd; a dwelling place for God. Just as Christ pitched his tent in the midst of humanity, so should the church live among all God's people. The church was to be a sign of pro-existence; an expression of God's utter, total love for all humanity.

So, gone were the aims, objectives, targets and measuring of outcomes. 'Just how do you measure God's activity?' asked Benedict of his congregation, in a sermon one Sunday. 'The church is not competing in a popularity contest, with Christianity hoping to win more customers and consumers in contemporary culture than other activities. Our faith is about sacrifice and service. Who knows, we might find we're at our best when we're faithful, not successful,' he argued. It made people think.

And Bishop Michael had watched this all unfold. It gave him just the smallest pang of pleasure to see the pendulum swing back, to a time long before *The Churchgoer's Charter* was launched.

But he knew it might swing again. Meanwhile, some lessons had been learnt.

A *parable*

There was a woman who lived on her own. She had no neighbours or close friends, but there was an old man who lived half a mile away. The woman had a house and a garden, and at the foot of a garden she had two apple trees that were her pride and joy. Once she was called away to see a sick relative. She gave the keys of the house to the old man, and asked him to check the house, but he was too infirm to tend the garden. She thought she would be away for a few days, but she was in fact gone for a few years.

From far away she heard of drought and storms, and she feared the worst. But when she did get home, things were pretty well as she had left them. She went into the garden, which was very overgrown, but the apple trees were still there – and in full bloom. She drank it all in, and her heart filled with delight and thanks.

Then she went to the tool shed, got out her pruners, went to the apple trees, and started to cut away at the dead wood. And she thought of the time when there would be apples for herself and for her neighbour.[46]

Part 4

Prayers and Poems

Readings and Poems

SYLVIA SANDS

BENT

Now he was teaching in one of the synagogues on the Sabbath. And just then there appeared a woman with a spirit that had crippled her for eighteen years. She was bent over and was quite unable to stand up straight. When Jesus saw her, he called her over and said, 'Woman, you are set free from your ailment.' When he laid his hands on her, immediately she stood up straight and began praising God. But the leader of the synagogue, indignant because Jesus had cured on the Sabbath, kept saying to the crowd, 'There are six days on which work ought to be done; come on those days and be cured, and not on the Sabbath day.' But the Lord answered him and said, 'You hypocrites! Does not each of you on the Sabbath untie his ox or his donkey from the manger, and lead it away to give it water? And ought not this woman, a daughter of Abraham whom Satan bound for eighteen long years, be set free from this bondage on the Sabbath day?' (Luke 13.10–16)

Dirt, ditches, dust,
Mud, blood, stones,
Weeds, scorpions, spittle,
Shadows, hooves, holes
And endless pairs of feet;
Your vista, your world view for eighteen years.
A voice
A call across a synagogue; words you had never hoped to hear,
'Woman, woman, woman,
You are released, you are liberated, you are free.'

Touch ... you had forgotten the feel, the comfort of:
Hands ... holding you, tracing that bent and twisted spine,
Jolting it, guiding it to straightness, to beauty, to dignity,
And oh, a face ...
Dark shadows beneath the eyes, deep lines towards the mouth,
'A man of sorrows and acquainted with grief'.
Love ... love come to claim and heal you,
Name you accurately 'Daughter of Abraham'.

All We are all at some time bent double, unable to straighten up;
Twisted caricatures of what we are meant to be,
Eyes seeing only dirt and darkness,
Life's detritus and despair.
Call to us through friends and families
Or through 'the kindness of strangers';
Touch us by hugs of humanity.
Straighten us, oh, straighten us to see
Your dear face again.

COMRADE

Again he entered the synagogue, and a man was there who had a withered hand. They watched him to see whether he would cure him on the Sabbath, so that they might accuse him. And he said to the man who had the withered hand, 'Come forward.' Then he said to them, 'Is it lawful to do good or to do harm on the Sabbath, to save life or to kill?' But they were silent. He looked around at them with anger; he was grieved at their hardness of heart and said to the man, 'Stretch out your hand.'

Perhaps it was the gradually softening calluses on his own palms
That caused Jesus to notice a fellow-artisan with a withered
   hand.
For in the remaining fragment of the Gospel to the Hebrews,
This man is revealed as a stone mason,
Rendered by accident or illness one of the great unemployed;
Unemployable.

Across the synagogue was there an intuitive moment of
   recognition?
Of quiet comradeship?
The carpenter and the stonemason ...
One longing for the weight and ring and strength and spark of
   stone,
The other, backward-yearning for the ordered, creative,
Safe and simple life of working with wood.
Brothers in loss.
All the mean-spirited crowd long for is that the carpenter
Should give them enough rope to hang him high.
'Go on,' they urge inwardly like ravening wolves, 'Heal him on
   the Sabbath'.
A wonder that they are not scorched by the anger and grief
Flaring up in that blazing, working man's heart of his!
Into their ice-cold silence he speaks, as is his wont,
To just one man's open heart,
'Stretch out your hand.'
And out of the synagogue, into the world,
Away from that calcified crowd they walk together,
The stonemason striding open-handed towards his future,
The carpenter edging towards the wood and nails of his past,
And the long evening shadows of a cross.

DUST

The scribes and the Pharisees brought a woman who had been
caught in adultery; and making her stand before all of them, they
said to him, 'Teacher, this woman was caught in the very act of
committing adultery. Now in the law Moses commanded us to
stone such women. Now what do you say?' They said this to
test him, so that they might have some charge to bring against
him. Jesus bent down and wrote with his finger on the ground.
When they kept on questioning him, he straightened up and said
to them, 'Let anyone among you who is without sin be the first to
throw a stone at her.' And once again he bent down and wrote on
the ground. (John 8.3–8)

Why on earth did he write on the ground ...?
Where else were her eyes focused if not cast down
Towards dirt.
The very least we expect from such women.
(Remember
Ruth Ellis
Christine Keeler
Pilloried Paula Yates)
'Be still,' came the unspoken message to her broken, terrified heart
From this unorthodox man doodling in the dust.
Such a playful thing to do given
The bloodthirsty, stone-throwing miasma in which he knelt.

Mind you – he is more than serious when upright again,
    speaking those straight-to-the-jugular words,
'Let the man who is without sin be the first to cast a stone at her.'

'He HAS to be manic-depressive!' we would judge,
From our psychiatry-in-five-easy-lessons sofas,
For down:
Like a clown he goes on his hunkers again,
Back to finger-painting and mud pies,
The Robin Williams of the Scriptures.
Some scholars suggest he was listing that cowardly crowd's sins
In large letters in the dirt they think she is.
It has the ring of truth.
Left alone together
To the sound of shifty retreating footsteps,
(No condemnation,
No judgement),
She sees for the first time in a man's eyes,
Her loveliness and dignity.

'GO!' he cries,
Launching her like a healed bird towards freedom.

GARDENER

But Mary stood weeping outside the tomb ... she turned round
and saw Jesus standing there, but she did not know that it was
Jesus. Jesus said to her, 'Woman, why are you weeping? For
whom are you looking?' Supposing him to be the gardener, she
said to him, 'Sir, if you have carried him away, tell me where you
have laid him, and I will take him away.' (John 20.11–15)

Down the centuries
People have preached at length about my error;
Some with pity, others with scorn.
(Typical over-emotional female – To think he was the
   GARDENER!)
Looking back,
He did not crash into the allotment of my life
But leaned on the gate gently;
Requesting entry.
First, he was the bin-man
Clearing out the accumulated rubbish
And putrid, rotting debris of my life
Hidden in the undergrowth.
Then he was the ploughman,
Furrowing, harrowing with his terrible love,
Slowly breaking up the foundations,
Breaking through to my good, rich soil.

Next, he was the sower,
Patiently, in wind and rain
And glorious sunshine
Scattering such tender, hopeful seeds
Into my deepest earth.
Finally, oh see! the flowers and heathers,
The shrubs and grasses,
The birds and butterflies,
The bursting, the blooming
Of my individual plot.
In hindsight,

I was doubly right among the tombs and terror,
The ruins and relics of that Morning.
I DID see,
I did recognize
My Beloved Gardener.

FEET

Jesus ... got up from the table, took off his outer robe, and tied
a towel around himself. Then he poured water into a basin and
began to wash the disciples' feet and to wipe them with the towel
that was tied around him ... After he had washed their feet, had
put on his robe and had returned to the table, 'Do you know what
I have done to you?' (John 13.3–12)

Not many people touch our feet;
Mothers; increasingly – fathers;
Later,
Lovers who claim to worship the ground we walk on.
Please note though, only mint-clean, spotless feet.
(I can remember kissing my sons' baby-feet,
Fresh after baths,
Blowing raspberries on the soles,
While their whole bodies shook with merriment at the sound.)

How long does it take
To wash twelve pairs of adult, dirty, male feet?
Enough to rid yourself of outer layers of clothes,
Lightened for the task.
Enough to make your back ache
And your hands go crinkly.
Long enough to tell the bones in your knees.

Long enough to add salty tears to dirty water
As gently, gently you take your leave of feet
That have followed faithfully.
(Even traitors')
For three long and dangerous years.

Was there ever an image as tender
As God saying, 'Farewell',
Stooped as a Mother with water, bowl, towel,
Over those funny, tired, individualistic, vulnerable dusty feet?

How long does it take
To cradle and wash
Twelve pairs of adult, dirty, male feet?

He probably made it last
As long as he could.

CENTURION

A centurion there had a slave whom he valued highly, and who
was ill and close to death. When he heard about Jesus, he sent
some Jewish elders to him, asking him to come and heal his slave.
When they came to Jesus, they appealed to him earnestly, saying,
'He is worthy of having you do this for him, for he loves our people, and it is he who built our synagogue for us.' And Jesus went
with them, but when he was not far from the house, the centurion
sent friends to say to him, 'Lord, do not trouble yourself, for I
am not worthy to have you come under my roof; therefore I did
not presume to come to you. But only speak the word, and let my
servant be healed' … When Jesus heard this he was amazed at
him, and turning to the crowd that followed him, he said, 'I tell
you, not even in Israel have I found such faith.' When those who
had been sent returned to the house, they found the slave in good
health. (Luke 7.2–10)

Here is a strange story …
A member of the occupying forces humbly asking help of
An itinerant Jewish Teacher who owns nothing
But the clothes he stands up in.
But then this Roman centurion loved the Jewish nation
And had even built them a synagogue.
Sometimes people tease me as an Englishwoman living

For thirty-six years in Ireland
'Sure, Sylvia – you're more Irish than the Irish!'
It happens.
Here is a challenging story ...
About a man loving another man,
And that person not his father or brother, cousin or son;
No,
Simply his employee, who the Gospel spells out bluntly was
'very dear to him'.

Here is a tender story ...
Of God responding to anyone who truly recognizes him,
Believes in his power and faithfulness,
Believes in a God
Who celebrates the love of a man for a man.

LEGION

And when he had stepped out of the boat, immediately a man
out of the tombs with an unclean spirit met him. He lived among
the tombs; and no one could restrain him any more, even with a
chain; for he had often been restrained with shackles and chains,
but the chains he wrenched apart, and the shackles he broke in
pieces; and no one had the strength to subdue him. Night and day
among the tombs and on the mountains he was always howling
and bruising himself with stones. When he saw Jesus from a distance, he ran and bowed down before him; and he shouted at the
top of his voice, 'What have you to do with me, Jesus, Son of the
Most High God? I adjure you by God, do not torment me.' For he
had said to him, 'Come out of the man, you unclean spirit!' Then
Jesus asked him, 'What is your name?' He replied, 'My name is
Legion; for we are many' ... Now there on the hillside a great
herd of swine was feeding; and the unclean spirits begged him,
'Send us into the swine; let us enter them.' So he gave them permission. And the unclean spirits came out and entered the swine;
and the herd, numbering about two thousand, rushed down the
steep bank into the lake. (Mark 5.2–13)

Safe in psychiatric hospital,
I had placed four friendly plastic bags,
Which once held loving gifts of fruit,
Chocolates, magazines, flowers.
Firmly over my head
In the cloakroom of the locked ward.
Like Legion, I wrestled with the demons
Tramp, tramp, tramping through my brain.
A legion was a Roman regiment of
Six thousand troops.
Show me a more accurate picture of mental illness.

After my failed cloakroom debacle on the ward,
The self-harming (... razors, needles, fire ...)
Young girls, aged from fourteen to twenty-one,
And I were drawn irresistibly together,
Our hollow eyes locked in a nightmare of understanding.
They mothering my ageing self with
Hugs, toffees under my pillow,
Carefully drawn pictures,
The delicate offering of painting my fingernails
In shocking pink.
Caught tears at two in the morning.
Legion, in among the tombs, watched his demons
Crashing via two thousand pigs over the Gadarene cliffs;
The relief of it! echoed later as he sits,
Clothed and in his right mind,
Calmly,
By the side of Jesus.
Who is to say that an echoing miracle was not begun in my mind,
(But slowly),
By that small regiment of unlikely,
Oh-so-young, self-scarred angels
In the locked ward?
After all,
Here I am, sitting quietly, writing poetry once more.

A Psalm and Reading for Each Day of the Week

JIM COTTER

Sunday

From an unfolding of Psalm 103

Just as parents are merciful to their children, so are you merciful
    and kind towards me.
For you know how fragile I am,
that I am made of the dust of the earth.
My days are like the grass,
they bloom like the flowers of the field:
the wind blows over them and they are gone,
and no one can tell where they stood.
Only your merciful goodness endures;
age after age you act justly
towards all who hold on to your covenant,
who take your words to heart and fulfill them.

From Hosea

A change of heart moves you, Beloved,
tenderness kindles within you.
You will not let loose with fury,
or come to me with threats.
For you are divine, and not human:
You are the Holy One,
present to me, intimate within me.
Thus I believe of the Living One:

You will lead me into the desert,
you will lure me into the wilderness.
And you will speak to my heart there,
with words of great tenderness.

Monday

From an unfolding of Psalm 23

Living One, you sustain me and feed me:
like a shepherd you guide me.
You lead me to an oasis of green, to lie down by restful waters.
Quenching my thirst, you restore my life: renewed and refreshed,
    I follow you,
a journey on the narrowest of paths.
Even when cliffs loom out of the mist,
my step is steady because of my trust.
Even when I go through the deepest valley,
with the shadow of darkness and death,
I shall fear no evil or harm.
For you are with me to give me strength,
your crook, your staff, at my side.
Even in the midst of my troubles,
with the murmurs of those who disturb me,
I know I can feast in your presence.
Your loving kindness and mercy
will meet me every day of my life.
By your Spirit you dwell within me,
and in the whole world around me,
and I shall abide in your house,
content in your presence for ever.

From Isaiah

Gently turning again, I breathe more freely.
Quietly waiting and trusting, my inner strength grows.

Tuesday

From an unfolding of Psalm 16

I give you thanks for the wisdom of your counsel, even at night
    you have instructed my heart.
In the silence of the darkest of hours
I open my ears to the whisper of your voice.
I have set your face always before me,
in every cell of my being you are there.
As I tremble on the narrowest of paths,
the steadying of your hand gives me courage.
Fleet of foot, with my eyes on the goal,
headlong in the chasm I shall not fall.
Therefore my heart rejoices and my spirit is glad, my whole
    being will rest secure.
For you will not give me over to the power of death, nor let your
    faithful ones see the pit.
You will show me the path of life:
in your countenance is the fullness of joy.
From the spring of your heart flow rivers of delight, a fountain
    of water that shall never run dry.

From the Gospel according to St Matthew

I shall not ask anxiously,
What am I to eat?
What am I to drink?
What shall I wear? ...
I shall set my heart and mind
on the divine commonwealth first,
and all the rest will come to me as well ...
So I shall not be anxious about tomorrow.
Today has enough problems of its own.
Tomorrow can look after itself ...

Wednesday

From an unfolding of Psalm 139

Light of light,
you have searched me out and known me.
You know where I am and where I go,
you see my thoughts from afar.
You discern my paths and my resting places,
you are acquainted with all my ways.
Where shall I go from your Spirit,
where shall I flee from your presence?
If I should cry to the darkness to cover me,
and the night to enclose me,
the darkness is no darkness to you,
and the night is as clear as the day.
For you have created every part of my being,
cell and tissue, blood and bone.
You know me to the very core of my being; nothing in me was
    hidden from your eyes
when I was formed in silence and secrecy,
in intricate splendour in the depths of the earth. Even as they
were forming you saw my limbs, each part of my body shaped
by your finger.
How deep are your thoughts to me,
how great is the sum of them.

From the Gospel according to St John

May I abide in you and you in me:
as the branch cannot bear fruit of itself, unless it abides in the
    vine,
neither can I unless I abide in you.

Peace you leave with me, your peace you give to me. Let not my
    heart be troubled, neither let me be afraid.

Thursday

From an unfolding of Psalm 91

Because you are bound to me in love,
therefore you will deliver me.
You will lift me out of danger
because I hold on to your name.
You know me in intimate trust,
in my inner heart I am loyal and true.
In my anguish and need you are with me,
you will set me free and clothe me with glory.

From St Paul

According to the riches of the divine glory,
may I be strengthened with might
through the Holy Spirit in my inner being,
that being rooted and grounded in love,
I may have power to comprehend, with all the saints, what is the
breadth and length and height and depth, and to know the deep
love which surpasses knowledge, that I may be filled with all the
fullness
of the One whose love is enduring and endless.

Friday

From an unfolding of Psalm 130

Empty, exhausted, and ravaged,
in the depths of despair I writhe.
Anguished and afflicted, terribly alone,
I trudge a bleak wasteland, devoid of all love.
In the echoing abyss I call out:
there is nothing but silence in return
Yet still I pray, Open your heart,
for my tears well up within me.

If you keep account of all that drags me down, there is no way I
   can stand firm.
Paralysed and powerless, I topple over,
bound by the evil I hate.
But with you is forgiveness and grace,
there is nothing I can give – it seems like a death. The power of
   your love is so awesome:
I am terrified by your freeing embrace.
Drawn from the murky depths by a fish hook,
I shout to the air that will kill me:
Must I leave behind all that I cherish
before I can truly breathe free?

From St Paul

Though my outer self is wasting away,
my inner self is being renewed every day.
For this slight momentary affliction
is preparing me for an eternal weight of glory beyond comparison,
because I look not to the things that are seen,
but to the things that are unseen;
for the things that are seen are transient,
but the things that are unseen are eternal.

Saturday

From an unfolding of Psalm 130

As a watchman waits for the morning,
through the darkest and coldest of nights,
more than the watchman who peers through the gloom,
I hope for the dawn, I yearn for the light.
You will fulfill your promise to bring me alive, overflowing with
   generous love.
You will free me from the grip of evil,
Loving One, merciful and compassionate.
Touching and healing the whole of my being,

you are a God whose reach has no limit.
All that has been lost will one day be found:
the communion of the rescued will rejoice in your name.

From the First Letter to Timothy

The Eternal One has not given me a spirit of fear, but of power
and of love and of a sound mind.

Poems and Prayers

SYLVIA SANDS

LOVE YOUR ENEMIES

Neither condemn nor destroy your enemies. Keep in contact
 with them –
even when you cannot keep 'in touch'.
Strive powerfully with them, struggling shoulder to shoulder,
 until you see each other face to face.
Be angry with compassion, not with hatred: Do not yield to
 bitterness or fury.
Be strongly and persuasively gentle – with others and with
 yourself.
Where there is icy hatred in your heart, let it be melted by the
 Spirit of Love.
Do not meet oppression with violation – for we have all been
 too much hurt.
Your enemies are human beings like yourself: do not picture
 them as less than human.
And keep a sense of proportion – and a sense of humour.
With expanding heart, *love* your enemies.

LOVE'S PERSISTENCE

Love is patient and kind and knows no envy.
Love never clings,
is never boastful, conceited, or rude. Love is never selfish,
never insists on its own way. Love is not quick to take offence.

Love keeps no score of wrongs, nor gloats over the sins of
others. Love rejoices in the truth.
Love is tough:
there is nothing it cannot face.
Love never loses trust
in human beings or in God. Love never loses hope, never loses
    heart.
Love still stands
when all else has fallen.

THE ADVERBS OF LOVE

Love others, and receive their love – passionately, on wings
of flame; fiercely, eager for truth; honestly, without illusion;
courageously, bearing the hurts; gently, with no hint of cruelty;
sensitively, giving room to breathe;
respectfully, without possessing;
responsibly, aware of consequence;
trustfully, without fear of rejection; welcomingly, without
demanding change; forgivingly, open to being reconciled;
generously, without thought of return; wholeheartedly, full of
faith and loyalty.

DWELLING IN LOVE

If you dwell in the Divine Love,
if you join the Dance of the Trinity,
the Lover, the Beloved, and the Mutual Friend, if you are caught
    up in the Love
that is generous and overflowing,
you will find yourself loving and being loved with the whole of
    your being,
loving your neighbour as yourself, and loving even your enemy;

and, as surely as night follows day, you will never use force –
though you will refuse to let others escape from love and truth;

you will never use others merely to provide what you want –
though you will respect and acknowledge your own needs;
you will never take advantage of others' ignorance or immaturity –
though you will try to increase their knowledge and wisdom.

within me ... and among us all ... as evolving life.
energy and light ... stardust and matter ... blood and breath ...
   flesh and feeling ...
ever-expanding consciousness ... within each cell ...
within each body ...
microcosm of the universe ... cosmic in destiny ...

AN UNFOLDING OF PART OF ISAIAH 43.1–4

You have created me
and you continue to shape me ...

You have rescued me
and you are liberating me ...

You have brought me a measure of healing, and you are
   restoring me ...

You call me by name,
and I belong to you ...
You are present with me on my journey ... When I wade
   through turbulent water,
the waves will not drown me ...

When I struggle against the wind,
the gusts will not throw me down ...

When I walk through fire,
the flames will not consume me ...

For you are the Living One, loving me beyond compare,
as the most precious jewel in your sight, honouring me beyond
   deserving ...

Again and again you reassure me: Do not be afraid ...

A PRAYER OF THANKSGIVING

Inspired by the General Thanksgiving in the Book of
Common Prayer

Eternal One, always alive and unconditionally loving,
giver of all good gifts,
we your friends and servants
now give you humble and hearty thanks
for all your goodness and loving kindness to us and to all the
    world.
We bless you for our creation, preservation,
and all the blessings of this life

We thank you for this new day, to be lived to the full ...
We thank you for this past day, pausing to reflect ... Above all,
we thank you for your great love
in the repairing and restoring of the world
through our liberator, reconciler, and healer Jesus Christ, for the
    means of grace
and for the hope of glory. And we ask of you,
give us that due sense of all your mercies,
that our hearts may be unreservedly thankful,
and that we show forth your praise,
not only with our lips but with our lives,
by giving up ourselves to your service,
and by walking before you
in compassion and righteousness all our days,
open always to your gift of holiness
through the narrow gate of Jesus Christ, who draws us through
    the needle's eye
and releases us into wide open spaces of freedom,
to whom with you and the Holy Spirit
be all gratitude and glory,
now and for ever. Amen.

A PRAYER OF TRUST

Inspired by Charles de Foucauld

AbbaAmma, Beloved Friend ...
I abandon myself into your hands ... In your *love* for me,
weave your will into the fabric of my life ...

Whatever that may bring, and wherever that may lead,
give me the courage to be steadfast and the grace to be
   thankful ...

Prepare me to be ready for all, to accept all that comes ...

Let only your will be done in me,
as in all life in this evolving universe, and I will ask nothing
   else ...

Into your hands
I commend the whole of my life ...

For I love you,
Loving Presence in my heart, and so I need to give ...

Steady my will to lay aside my surface self
and to let my deep self be the centre of my being ...

trusting you without reserve ...
For you are faithfully creating me ...
making me, repairing me, transforming me ...
AbbaAmma, Beloved Friend ...

This is the hardest part of this journal that I can no longer post-
pone writing. I need to express – in so far as I can – something of
the ghastly time spent in hospital over Christmas and New Year. I
would not wish this on anyone and fervently hope never to experience the like again.

   To help keep the nausea at bay during the first days of each
chemo cycle, after I'd not kept any food down for a couple of
days in the first cycle, I was prescribed, in good faith, a drug called

aprepitant. It worked fine on the nausea, but it has the fairly uncommon side effect of producing hallucinations. The dose I took in early October and November did not trouble me, but that in December did. Perhaps combined with the effect of the chemo cocktail on my system overall, I began to feel weary and hopeless and in an increasingly dark place. I don't have much memory of the second and third weeks of the month, but my condition began to concern those around me. Anxious and confused, beginning to experience delusions that I was convinced were real, I was – for the second time – taken into hospital by ambulance, I think on 20 December. One of my delusions was that somehow the laws of the universe had changed, and that nobody had control over their vehicles on the road. All was crash and chaos, and I remember feeling astonished that the ambulance driver was having no problem getting to Bangor and that the street lights were working. As with the consequences of taking the steroids, I had increasingly over the previous days found it harder and harder to speak. This time I was reduced to saying, paradoxically, 'I can't speak.' I could say those words but no others.

I do have some clear memories of my arrival at the hospital, not least because G was there, expecting to be able, on my behalf, to talk with the medical staff. I remember being taken to Tryfan, the admission ward, and the doctor on duty. I was agitated, angry, and anxious, and found it

Christ crucified

Christ crucified,

nailed to the unyielding wood,
bearer to me of the true and living God, give me courage to face
   what must decay,

the disintegration of my mortal flesh,

and give me faith to shed my false and deadly self, to let it be as
smoke vanishing in the evening breeze, that as soul-body I may
grow through all my days refined to a finer tuning than I can yet
discern,

shaped into the likeness of your transfigured, risen body, that my
    true and lively self,
fresh embodied,

a living flame at last,

may dwell and dance with you, in love, for ever:

Going through a narrow gate

To go through a narrow gate,

a needle's eye,

is to accept

constriction, restraint, limitation.
There is only one way left.

Now is the time to take my unique path,

a path along which there will be a dying.

Nothing will ever be the same again. There is no way back.
But there is a way through.

The Candle Trilogy

Unlit betrayal

At the top
Is the water source
So pure
The priest takes
A bottle full
Puts a stopper in
In the valley
The church of
Bottled water
Dispenses
Drop by drop
Meagre blessings
Wondering why
The children
Are missing
Is it that they know
Water falls
In a cascade
A torrent
For everyone
In the valley
And the river's
Been pissed in
By the Mayor?
Who reneged
Cheated

The Pied Piper
The flute now
Lures the children
To be lost
Under a mountain of
Indebted
Hopelessness
Rats return
Gnawing the candle
Of their dreams
But every child
Dares to light
That candle
They do it
Behind their
Parents' backs
Placing it in a holder
Sincerely
Wishing for flame
Hopeful
That the flickering light
Will make them sacred
They doubt it
Their snuffing fingers
Warm wax rubbing
Worried they'll
Be revealed by
Tainting scent
The candle now unlit
Irresolute, they chance
No accidental fire
But will you
Give them
A match?

(It is said that in 1284 the Pied Piper of Hamlin was retained to get rid of
the rats and drowned them all. Then the Mayor reneged on the bill and the
Pied Piper lured away all but three of the town's children.)

Lit faithfulness

It's simpler
Than you think
No mountains
To climb
No epiphanies
To have
No words
To preach
Just buy a box of
Matches
It does not matter
Who you meet
Or what they
Believe
Each has a candle of
Cherished dreams
Invite everyone
Out of the rain
Out of the wind
Out of the sun
Just enough shelter
To pause
Most will not
Stop
They'll just
Brush you by
Too busy
Too harried
Too ambitious
Too broken
If they give you
The time of day
Ask 'Where's
Your candle?'
Your ask will restore
Candles

Eaten by rats
Long hidden
Denied
Forgotten
Ask who
Rains on them
Blows out their light
Glares too bright
Then give them
The box of matches
Let them
Strike the light
If needed
Cup your hands
Protect the wick
As they
Light the candle
Of their dreams
Let the flickering
Grow to flame
Now listen to them in
Their sacred space
Hear the tales of their
Cherished dreams
Ask
'Is it lit?'
At 'yes'
You leave behind
Matches
Not thinking

Faithful betrayal – Holy Fire

First of the Trinity

Mary

God does not
Rape
Mary.
If God had raped Mary
Do you think we'd have her joy
So magnificently described?
God sends Gabriel
He appears as the most
Gorgeous of men.
She hugs him saying,
'You are so beautiful.'
Places her head on his chest,
Looks up
And tentatively
They kiss on the lips.
He moves to kiss her again.
'No,' she says,
'My betrothal is arranged.
My father is making me marry.
I cannot defy him,
My blood-line, my tribe.'
Gabriel steps back.
'You get to decide.
God's love is consensual.
Any other story
Is a lie made up
By man.'
Mary tremors at the idea.
A woman freed to choose
Love over tribe,
A woman no longer
Property of man
With the right to decide.

Knowing that this right is
The centre of God's love
For all mankind.
She chooses love.
She defies her dad,
She faithfully betrays her blood.
'Be it unto me
According to
Thy word ...'
Gabriel, Mary
As man
As woman
Fully alive
Feeling
Exploring
Adoring
Intertwining
Through each other
Combining
To be
Worship
To and from
Eternity
Now one
With God
Now spiralling
In a greater orbit
Knowing they are
Saying yes to life,
To Jesus.
She gives birth to a boy
Who grows to be a man
Who in time understands,
But before,
His tribe raises him
As their man.
Like all of us
He learns the normal

Basis of hate:
Who's in?
Who's out?
How is my blood superior?
I am a boy,
I am this belief and religion,
I am of my tribe.

Second of the Trinity

The Syrophoenician woman

He grows into a prophet,
Limited at first,
He prays to the Father,
And says he is just a man for
The lost sheep of his tribe.
One day he meets a woman,
A woman who says, 'No,
That is not good enough.'
She prays as a Mother,
The Mother who is
Desperate
For her sick child.
She is foreign,
Annoying, cloying
And totally persistent.
She is not of his blood,
Gender, race, tribe
Caste, class or God.
He denies her,
He reviles her,
Finally calls her a dog.
She faithfully sees past
The hate he's been taught
She knows his heart.
She stands her ground,
Tells him,

'Even dogs get scraps.'
Like flint
She strikes him,
Sparks his love.
She breaks the clasp that holds
His cultural coat of hate,
It falls away,
Revealing the loving heart
Given him
By his mother and God.
His mutual love flows,
He loves her daughter
As his own.
Free,
He heals
Into the Messiah.

Third of the Trinity

Mary Magdalene

He is now on the path
To be crucified
By those so superior.
Now he honours every woman,
Every foreigner,
Every other.
Now he's got it,
Are you surprised
Why he is such a hit
With all the women
Of the Gospels
Described?
Are you surprised
That those of power,
Still dressed in hate,
Come after him
For such betrayal

With bloodshed in mind?
Betrayed by a kiss,
Led through the crowds,
They kill him on a tree.
Mary Magdalene
She watches him die.
His agony consumes her,
She struggles to stop
The terror
From petrifying her.
He dies. Is it over?
The light is fading fast
When his body is released.
She follows
As they take his body
To the tomb.
A new one carved into rock
With a circular stone
That rolls back into a slot.
They haul his body
Down into the antechamber
On to the preparation table,
No time
To put him into
One of the burial slots.
It is Sabbath,
Darkness,
She'll return when allowed.
On the third day
She comes early,
Still in darkness
With enough myrrh
To stop the retching
That celebrates
The victory of those
Who kill those who
Put love before blood.
The stone is sitting

In its slot
Rolled back.
No stench,
No body,
Another humiliating loss.
The rock-carved tomb,
The ultimate dead end,
Is emptiness.
Have the men of bloodshed
Desecrated his body
And hidden their evil deed?
'No!' she screams.
In the place of despair
She is faithful to love,
She feels it envelop her.
She turns, risen he is there,
Betraying death itself
Her love explodes,
It is that mutual love
It feels consensual
Beyond sexual,
Union with God.
No hatred to those who kill,
Compassion for all,
Resurrection love
From her pours forth.

Finally Holy Fire

Yes his act is sacred betrayal.
Yes his reward is death,
Yes he is going to ask you to
Stand with the poor,
Under the stars and
Light the candle of a little child.
You will light her candle
Regardless of who you are.
Free, you will not ask

Of gender
Of race
Of tribe
Of caste
Of class
Of God
You'll faithfully betray
Your tribe if you answer
Yes to what Jesus and
The Trinity of women ask,
'Are you flint enough
To light Holy Fire?'

Kingdom Come: Spartacus, Untamed

MARTYN PERCY

I want to travel back through time to around 70 BC, and then to about AD 70, to talk about rebellion and dissent as acts of freedom – as acts that radically express our humanity, and God's purpose for humanity: to be free.

So let me begin in 70 BC. The film *Spartacus* (1960, directed by Stanley Kubrick) needs little introduction for most people. Starring Kirk Douglas as the rebellious slave Spartacus, it is based on a historical novel by Howard Fast – and inspired by the real life of a Thracian slave who led the revolt in the Third Servile War of 73–71 BC. A small band of former gladiators and slaves, perhaps no more than 80 in number, and led by Spartacus, grew to an army of around 125,000, to challenge the might of the Roman empire. Kubrick's film starred Laurence Olivier as the Roman general-politician, Marcus Licinius Crassus. Peter Ustinov won an Academy Award for best supporting actor as Batiatus, a slave trader. Jean Simmons played the part of Varinia, a slave-woman and the lover of Spartacus, and Tony Curtis played the slave Antonius.

Less well known is the film's own story of rebellion. The screenwriter Dalton Trumbo, along with several other Hollywood writers, had been blacklisted for his political beliefs, and associations with movements seeking equality for coloured and black people, as well as members of the American Communist Party, some of whom were jailed. Even though the age of McCarthyism was crumbling, it still took a young aspirational senator – John F. Kennedy – crossing the picket lines to see the film, to help end Trumbo's blacklisting. Howard Fast had also been blacklisted, and originally self-published his novel.

Looking back, we can see why Trumbo's script should perhaps have caused audiences to ponder some potential for subversive political messages. But there were more obvious, overt challenges to the establishment in the film.

For example, much of the United States was still colour-segregated in 1960. But we are introduced to Draba, a heroic black slave, first overpowering the white Spartacus in gladiatorial combat – and then sacrificing his own life in protest at the oppression of slaves. Equally unusual, for a Hollywood film of that era, was an ending that was both realistic and tragic – seemingly without hope.

The film also explores different kinds of love between men, which was rare for the time. There is the relationship between Spartacus and Antoninus, made to fight to the death by their Roman captors. The final words between them are Spartacus saying, 'Forgive me, Antoninus', to which the dying Antoninus replies, 'I love you, Spartacus ...' Earlier in the film, we find Crassus and his then slave, Antoninus, in a bathing scene – with the slave gently sponging and washing his master. The 'gay subtext' is pretty clear, with Crassus declaring his passion for both 'oysters and snails':

Crassus: Do you eat oysters?
Antoninus: When I have them, master.
Crassus: Do you eat snails?
Antoninus: No, master.
Crassus: Do you consider the eating of oysters to be moral and the eating of snails to be immoral?
Antoninus: No, master.
Crassus: Of course not. It is all a matter of taste, isn't it?
Antoninus: Yes, master.
Crassus: ... taste is not the same as appetite, [so] not a question of morals?
Antoninus: It could be argued so, master.
Crassus: My robe, Antoninus. My taste includes both snails and oysters.

Here, Trumbo's screenplay gives us an interesting excursion into moral philosophy. There is nothing wrong with taste (or orientation) according to Crassus; the ethical issue is the sating, or control, of appetite. Crassus' bisexuality in this scene – like others – carries subtle, seditious subtexts. The viewer of the film is being challenged on many levels: issues of race, sexuality, political hierarchy and slavery are all strongly featured in the screenplay. Yet most cinema-goers at the time would have missed these themes, explicitly. Although when we look at a lot of half-naked men, very fit, tanned and oiled, in gladiatorial combat – we do begin to wonder ...!

That said, many in the cinema audience might have perhaps sensed some of these themes implicitly. It was Kierkegaard who opined that 'life is lived forward, but understood backwards'. So it is unlikely that cinema-goers in the early 1960s picked up any subversive sublimation in the sub-plots. But, looking back, we can understand what Trumbo may have wanted to say at the dawn of a new decade, in a repressive social and political climate that was about to become progressively liberal.

Well, so much for 70 BC, but we can see why a film about an almost-successful slave-rebellion did not go down well in cinemas in the south of the United States in the 1960s when there was still colour segregation and, to a large extent, slavery. But what about such a theme in AD 70?

The gospel of Christ is radically inclusive: Jew, Greek, gentile, slave, free – all shall be welcome in the kingdom of God. So, what of Galatians 3.28–29: 'There is no longer Jew or Greek, there is no longer slave or free, there is no longer male and female; for all of you are one in Christ Jesus. And if you belong to Christ, then you are Abraham's offspring, heirs according to the promise'? If we could travel back in time to Paul's Colossae, we would notice, like any city of the day, that they were buzzing with cultural and ethnic diversity – much like cities today. But there were some crucial differences too. It was difficult to keep order in such cities. Cities, to be well ordered, were governed by assemblies. These were sometimes called *ekklesia* – an ancient commonplace secular word from which we derive the term 'church'. And to help keep order in cities, ethnic groups who were non-citizens often lived in neighbourhoods or ghettoes. Indeed, even in modern times, we find areas of a city – sometimes called 'quarters', such as a Latin Quarter, literally meaning places to stay – for Spaniards, French, Chinese; and sometimes for groups that are marginalized (e.g. Jewish ghetto). In ancient times, the areas reserved in a city for non-citizens were known as *paroikia* – from which we get the English word 'parish'. This is where the resident aliens lived; those who lived in the city contributed to its welfare, but had no voting rights as such.

In the churches that Paul knew, the *ekklesia* was complex. People gathered – they assembled; in itself, unusual for a religion. In the first churches, we find Jews, Greeks and Romans; slave and free; male and female. All one in Christ. The slaves are marked with tattoos; the children run free; the men and women mix; origin and ethnicity no longer matter, for all are one in Jesus Christ. In this radical new 'assembly' of non-citizens, all are equal. Class, race, gender and age are all transcended. The 'parish church', then, is the inside place for the outsider. Or, as William Temple once put it, the only club that exists for non-members. This is what it means to be one in Christ: built together to be the dwelling place of God; the *oikos* – 'God's household'. The body of Christ, indeed.

Churches rarely think about the origins of their identity in this radical way. They mostly go about their business assuming their values, and implicitly imbibing these from one generation to the next. In a way, this is a pity, as valuable practices are often left to chance: inchoate by nature, they simply persist implicitly. Churches rarely think, for example, about how and why they welcome the strangers and aliens in their midst – mostly very easily, and without fuss or further reflection. But welcome they do: not only giving to the stranger, but also receiving from them. This is not merely an observation about how Christians engage with others who are not kith and kin; it is also a remark about the oft-hidden dynamic of reception, gift and charity. So just how revolutionary is the Church?

To some extent, it is a pity that the term 'inclusive' today has become so bound up with a slightly tribal and 'liberal' identity. But perhaps this should not surprise us, for the word 'include' began its life with a fairly insular definition. Drawing from the Latin word *includere*, it means 'to shut in, enclose or imprison' – just as 'exclude' meant to 'shut out'.

But Jesus is not for either option. The defining character of the kingdom of God Jesus inaugurated draws from a rather richer word: *incorporate*. That is to say, to put something into the body or substance of something else; from the Latin *incorporare*, it means to 'unite into one body'. The kingdom of God, like the Church, was to be one of hybridity. This was a lesson Jesus learnt in his childhood, and embodied in adulthood. God brings us all together. He's all done with working through a single tribe or race. The Church that begins at Pentecost has been dress-rehearsed in Jesus' ministry: it will be multi-lingual, multi-cultural and multi-racial. It will be multiple. Yet we, though being many, are one body.

So, I am not for an exclusive Church, and I am not for membership of an inclusive Church. I am for Christ. When we look at Colossians 4, what do we find? A long list of names – foreign and local, Jew and Greek, slave and free, who are not part of a new tribe, but, rather, part of an international *ekklesia*. The Church is the outworking of Jesus' ministry. That's all the Church is. That's all ecclesiology is actually: our social and embodied response to what our theology is. Who we think Christ is tends to determine what kind of church we attempt to shape. That's why Paul exhorts us to 'Conduct yourselves wisely towards outsiders, making the most of the time. Let your speech always be gracious, seasoned with salt, so that you may know how you ought to answer everyone ...' (Colossians 4.5–6). Our evangelism, in other words, comes not just from our words, but also our goodness, and our character. We are called to be a good, open and welcoming body: the Church.

So what has Spartacus got to do with the Church of England, perplexed as it still is by questions of sexuality? The social changes in the last decades have caught the Church off guard, and on the defensive. While the nation has often turned its face towards justice, integrity and equality, our senior Church leaders have turned the other way. The confident national Church of the 1960s and 1970s – often producing senior clergy at the forefront of progressive social change on decriminalizing homosexuality or divorce laws, for example – gave way to a more circumspect Church in the closing years of the twentieth century.

While our nation offered sanctuary to people persecuted for their sexuality, seeking asylum from overseas, many senior leaders have slowly kettled the Church into behaving like a wary sect on the subject of sexuality. It's ironic that much of this 'leadership' largely consists of nervous silence. Underlying this has been enormous confusion in the Church concerning the relationship between secularism and liberalism. But they are quite different. Secularism marginalizes religion. Liberalism, however, has deep and profound roots in progressive, orthodox Christianity, which are found in the teachings of Jesus and his disciples – equality, justice and liberation being just some of the values that the early Church embodied, and sought to extend to the wider society.

The capacity of our Church leaders to grasp the opportunities in society today – for renewed mission and ministry in the context of complex changes within our culture for example – have often been egregiously spurned. Our crusading conservatism has left the Church looking self-righteous, sour, mean-spirited and isolated. In his prescient *Refounding the Church*,[46] Gerry Arbuckle argues that dissenters in society not only have rights, but also duties. He notes with care how Jesus, as a principled dissenter, challenged the status quo with patience, tolerance and love. He also argues that dissent is an essential component in mission – a mission that witnesses to the world, and also converts the Church.

But Jesus is more than a dissenter because he takes on the suffering and affliction of the individuals he cures, such that it becomes part of him. This view would not have been strange to the early Church Fathers, whose progressive move towards a richly incarnational theology required them to conclude that what was not assumed could not be redeemed. So, Jesus risks social ostracization when he dines with Zacchaeus, consorts with sinners, and receives women of dubious repute into his company, precisely in order to take on their brokenness, as well as take on the taboos of society that maintain structures that divorce the secular and sacred.

As Janet Soskice has pointed out,[47] it is no different in the healing miracles themselves. Noting the story of the haemorrhaging woman in Luke 8.40–56 (cf. Mark 5.21–43 and Matthew 9.18–34), she points out that what is striking about it is Jesus' willingness to touch or be touched by an 'impure' woman. Although modern readers of the text may find this aspect of the narrative hard to relate to, the significance of Jesus' action should not be underestimated: the woman defiled the teacher which, according to Levitical law, she would have done for she was in a state of permanent uncleanness, polluting everyone and everything with whom she came into contact. Her poverty – 'she had spent all she had' – is a direct result of her affliction.

Yet Jesus, apart from healing her, also seems to challenge the social and religious forces that have rendered this woman 'contagious'. He calls her 'daughter' in all three accounts, and all three evangelists stress the woman's faith. Interestingly, the synoptic accounts of the haemorrhaging woman are all paired with the raising of Jairus' daughter. Again, the issues of impurity (touching a corpse) and of menstruation occur: the girl is 12, and her untimely death clearly prevents her from entering womanhood. Jesus declares her 'not dead, but sleeping', and his touch, resulting in his defilement, raises the girl.

The work of the literary critic Frank Kermode has important resonances with the observations made by Soskice. Kermode's discussion of the purity issues in Mark 5 picks up on the fact that the stories of the haemorrhaging woman and Jairus' daughter have been paired and conflated. Kermode cites as evidence for this the undue prominence Mark gives to the narrative by the sharing of the number 'twelve' (the girl is 12, and the woman has also been ill for 12 years): 'this coincidence signifies a narrative relation of some kind between the woman and the girl ... an older woman is cured of a menstrual disorder of twelve years' standing, and is sent back into society. A girl who has not yet reached puberty is reborn ...'[48]

Kermode presses his claim that the narrative is centred on gender-related taint with some force: 'they take their complementary ways out of sickness into society, out of the unclean into the clean'. Jesus does not negate either of the women, nor does he 'demonize' their afflictions, or imply that they are unclean – the healing comes from their being accepted by him as they are: their 'defilement' is done away with.

Modern readers might well struggle with these texts, and wonder what all the fuss is about in relation to normal issues in 'feminine hygiene'. But contemporary society may not be quite as progressive as it imagines. The story of how the Samaritans began – the organization founded in 1953 by the Reverend Chad Varah – has some resonance with the story of Jairus' daughter.

Varah's inspiration came from an experience he had had as a young curate in the city (and diocese) of Lincoln. Varah had taken a funeral for a girl of 14 who had killed herself because she had begun menstruating, and was mortified that this girl had to be buried in unconsecrated ground, with parts of the burial liturgy redacted as it was a suicide. Varah became concerned about the state of sex education for teenagers in the city, and started to work with young people, especially listening to those who were contemplating suicide. Varah's Samaritan movement grew rapidly when he subsequently moved to London. Within ten years, the Samaritans were a sizeable charity, offering a supportive and empathetic listening service that is not political or religious.

So, the story of Jairus' daughter and that of the older woman (both women, we note, are un-named) are remarkable. The pairing of these two stories seems to turn everything around. A woman becomes a daughter, and a daughter becomes a woman. Moreover, we might also allow ourselves a little speculation. What precisely is the relationship between Jairus and the bleeding woman? Remember, Jairus is the Synagogue Ruler, and would therefore have an instrumental role in policing its precincts, keeping the impure and undesirable out. So now we have a story about immediacy and patience. The woman has waited for 12 years – and has probably been excluded from worship for the same period of time. One of the subtle yet blunt exercises of power is to make people wait, or be kept waiting.

If you are in power, people wait to see you – or you keep them waiting; it is the powerless who must wait. For that appointment, the letter, the news, the interview – waiting is a form of powerlessness. Jairus kept this woman waiting for years; but he wants Jesus to heal his daughter, *now*. What does Jesus do? He gets distracted by an apparently pointless brush with a member of the crowd, and keeps Jairus waiting – and for too long too.

Where is the lesson in this? This is a miracle with a moral. So, we are now in a position to understand the significance of Jesus' encounter with the two women and their 'healing' or, indeed, understand why Jesus bothered with lepers. When, in the midst of the dynamics of this particular understanding of the relationship between an 'impure' body and the social body, Jesus reaches out and *touches* the unclean and declares them healed, he acts as an alternative boundary keeper in a way that is religiously and ritually subversive to the customs of society. He disrupts and undermines the social order that declares such people outcasts. Therefore, Jesus makes possible a new community that now refuses to be founded upon the exclusion of the other.

And so to return to *Spartacus*. As the film closes, Crassus tries to identify his nemesis amid the slaughtered remains and remnant of the crushed slave rebellion; the surviving comrades of Spartacus stand as one to proclaim, 'I am Spartacus'. And we all are Spartacus, if we refuse to stand by and see others crushed. Like Spartacus' slave army, there are millions more Christians who simply say 'not in my name' will the Church oppress you. Oppress my gay brother and lesbian sister in Christ, and you oppress me. I would rather die free than live under oppression.

The human spirit will not be crushed. Tyranny will not triumph. There is beautiful, loving solidarity abiding in our shared, deepest dissent. Surely it is better to die free than live enslaved? Yet some will point to how the film *Spartacus* finishes. The hero is cruelly forced to take the life of his dearest companion in a hastily organized duel-to-the-death. For the 'victor', only crucifixion awaits – with thousands of others along the Appian Way. And there the rebellion ends; as might the story.

But Kubrick's epic has one more scene. The slave-woman Varinia, the lover of Spartacus, and with whom she has now borne a son, escapes from the clutches of Crassus through the intervention of Batiatus, the former slave trader. Leaving Rome in disguise, they pass Spartacus, dying on his cross. Varinia holds up their son to his face, and simply proclaims, 'He is free, Spartacus; he is free.' The rebellion, it would seem, is vindicated. As the film hints, we only truly live by looking forward. As a Church, we only understand how far we have travelled when we look back. But live forward we must.

The Lord was, is, and always will be with us – until we see his kingdom come, his will be done – on earth as it is in heaven. Until then, I am Spartacus. So are you. Untamed by a Church that would enslave – by silence, oppression and denial – all those who, made in the image of God, have been made to feel that they are not normal, and therefore do not truly belong. So, whether we live or die, the result was never in any doubt. We shall ultimately live as God intends – as full, free and equal citizens in this community we know as the Church, and for the sake of the coming of the kingdom.

Notes and References

1 Martyn Percy *et al.*, *The Bright Field: Readings, Reflections and Prayers for Ascension, Pentecost, Trinity and Ordinary Time*, Norwich: Canterbury Press, 2014, Jim Cotter *et al.*, *Darkness Yielding: Liturgies, Prayers and Reflections for Christmas, Holy Week and Easter*, Norwich: Canterbury Press, 2004.

2 John Hull, *In the Beginning There Was Darkness: A Blind Person's Conversations with the Bible*, London: SCM Press, 2010.

3 Harvey Cox, *On Not Leaving it to the Snake*, London: SCM Press, 1968.

4 Lytta Bassett, *Holy Anger: Jacob, Job, Jesus*, London: Continuum, 2007.

5 Tim Wyatt, 'Survivors' Protest aided by Chapter', *Church Times*, 7 October 2016.

6 'The Thin Red Line' was a phrase coined by a journalist of *The Times* to refer to Scottish Highland troops resisting a Russian cavalry charge at the Battle of Balaclava in the Crimea in 1854. The title was later borrowed by James Jones for his 1962 fictional account of warfare between the American and Japanese troops in 1942. Its only relevance is that it refers to soldiers in battle.

7 John Paul Lederach, *The Moral Imagination: The Art and Soul of Building Peace*, Oxford: Oxford University Press, 2010.

8 Lesley Hunter, *The Seed and the Fruit*, London: SCM Press, 1953.

9 Hunter, *The Seed and the Fruit*, p. 12.

10 Norman Vincent Peale, *The Power of Positive Thinking*, New York: Schuster & Schuster, 1952.

11 Aurelian Crăiuţu, *Faces of Moderation: The Art of Balance in an Age of Extremes*, Philadelphia PA: University of Pennsylvania Press, 2017.

12 Aurelian Crăiuţu, *A Virtue for Courageous Minds: Moderation in French Political Thought, 1748–1830*, Princeton NJ: Princeton University Press, 2016.

13 Ian McEwan, *Atonement*, London: Vintage Books, 2002, p. 371.

14 McEwan, *Atonement*, p. 372. My italics.

15 John Boyne, *The Boy in the Striped Pyjamas*, London: Random House, 2006.

16 Stanley Hauerwas, ed., *Growing Old in Christ*, Grand Rapids MI: Eerdmans, 2003.

17 Anne Lamott, *Traveling Mercies*, New York: Anchor Books, 1999.

18 Die Gedenkstätte deutscher Widerstand, Stauffenbergstrasse, 13–14, Berlin.

19 Helmuth James von Moltke, *Letters to Freya: A Witness against Hitler*, London: Collins-Harvill, 1991, p. 175.

20 von Moltke, *Letters to Freya*, p. 60.

21 von Moltke, *Letters to Freya*, p. 409.

22 Philip Larkin, *The Whitsun Weddings*, London: Faber & Faber, 1964.

23 From the film written by Bruce Joel Rubin, *Jacob's Ladder*, 1990.

24 Dan Brown, *The Da Vinci Code*, New York: Doubleday, 2003, chapter 55.

25 Elizabeth Barrett Browning, *Aurora Leigh*, 1856. See Elizabeth Barrett Browning, *Aurora Leigh*, Oxford: Oxford University Press (Oxford World's Classics), 2008.

26 Brian McLaren, *A Generous Orthodoxy*, Grand Rapids MI: Zondervan, 2006.

27 Adapted from a piece in *Modern Believing*, vol. 36, no. 1, 1995.

28 Les Murray, *Translations from the Natural World*, Manchester: Carcanet Press, 1992.

29 John Lindqvist, *Let the Right One In*, New York: St Martin's Press, 2004.

30 David Walker, 'An Angelic Salutation' (unpublished). Reproduced here with permission.

31 Larry Keefauver, *Angels on Command*, Newberry FL: Bridge Logos, 2004.

32 Polycarp, AD 155, *Acts of the Christian Martyrs* ('Martyrium Polycarpi' – *9.3; 21, Acta Martyrum*).

33 Clifford Geertz, *The Interpretation of Cultures*, New York: Basic Books, 1973.

34 The Venerable Bede, *History of the English Church and People*, trans. L. Shirley-Price, London: Penguin Classics, 1991.

35 Bede, *History of the English Church*, I.1.

36 Bede, *History of the English Church*, II.1.

37 *Bede: On the Temple*, Liverpool: Liverpool University Press, 1955, I.1.

38 George Herbert, *Herbert: The Complete English Works* (Everyman's Library), London: Everyman, 1996.

39 John Macmurray, *Persons in Relation*, New York: Humanity Books, 1998.

40 Harold S. Kushner, *When Bad Things Happen to Good People*, New York: Anchor Books, 2004 edn.

41 Reinhold Niebuhr, 'The Serenity Prayer'. See Fred Shapiro, 'I Was Wrong about the Origin of the Serenity Prayer', 15 May 2015 (http://www.huffingtonpost.com/2014/05/15/serenity-prayer-origin_n_5331924.html).

42 James Rebanks, *The Shepherd's Life: A Tale of the Lake District*, London: Allen Lane, 2015.

43 Urban T. Holmes, *What is Anglicanism?*, New York: Morehouse Publishing, 1982, p. 95.

44 The story was originally published in *Signs of the Times*, Lent 1992, and in a revised form in *Modern Believing*, July 2011, with the addition of the Postscript. In its current form it has also appeared in Martyn Percy, *The Ecclesial Canopy*, London: Ashgate, 2014, pp. 198, 204.

45 See www.theguardian.com/world/2015/nov/21/justin-welby-church-england-new-synod.

46 Gerry Arbuckle, *Refounding the Church*, New York: Orbis Books, 1996.

47 Janet Soskice. I am indebted to Dr Janet Soskice for some of these insights, in her (unpublished) paper 'Blood and Defilement', given at the Annual Society for the Study of Theology Conference, 1994.

48 Frank Kermode, *The Genesis of Secrecy: On the Interpretation of Narrative*, Cambridge MA: Harvard University Press, 1979.